D1414452

Toward the Prevention of Alcohol Problems

Government, Business, and Community Action

Dean R. Gerstein, *editor*

Summary of a conference held under
the auspices of the

Panel on Alternative Policies
Affecting the Prevention of Alcohol Abuse and Alcoholism

Commission on Behavioral and Social Sciences and Education

National Research Council

NATIONAL ACADEMY PRESS
Washington, D.C. 1984

National Academy Press ● 2101 Constitution Avenue, NW ● Washington, DC 20418

Library of Congress Cataloging in Publication Data

International Standard Book Number 0-309-03485-X

Printed in the United States of America

Steering Group
Conference on
Alcohol Policy Research

MARK H. MOORE *(Chair)*, John F. Kennedy School of Government, Harvard University

DAN E. BEAUCHAMP, Department of Health Policy and Administration, School of Public Health, University of North Carolina

HOWARD BLANE, Department of Rehabilitation Counselling, Graduate School of Education, University of Pittsburgh

SHEILA BLUME, Sayville, New York (formerly Medical Director, National Council on Alcoholism)

PHILIP COOK, Institute of Policy Sciences and Public Affairs and Department of Economics, Duke University

JOHN DOYLE, Chairman of the Board of Directors, National Council on Alcoholism, New York

MARILYN GOLDWATER, House of Delegates, Maryland General Assembly

ANNE LINDEMAN, Arizona State Senate

DONALD MCCONNELL, Commission on Alcohol and Drug Abuse, State of Connecticut

JAMES F. MOSHER, Prevention Research Group, Medical Research Institute of San Francisco, and Prevention Research Center, Pacific Institute for Research and Education

FRANK RAFLO, Board of Supervisors, County of Loudoun, Virginia

ROBERT STRAUS, Department of Behavioral Sciences, School of Medicine, University of Kentucky

Panel on Alternative Policies Affecting the Prevention of Alcohol Abuse and Alcoholism

MARK H. MOORE *(Chair)*, John F. Kennedy School of Government, Harvard University

GAIL BURTON ALLEN, Department of Psychiatry, St. Luke's-Roosevelt Hospital Center, New York

DAN E. BEAUCHAMP, Department of Health Policy and Administration, School of Public Health, University of North Carolina

PHILIP COOK, Institute of Policy Sciences and Public Affairs and Department of Economics, Duke University

JOHN KAPLAN, School of Law, Stanford University

NATHAN MACCOBY, Institute for Communication Research, Stanford University

DAVID MUSTO, Child Study Center and Department of History, Yale University

ROBIN ROOM, School of Public Health, University of California, Berkeley, and Medical Research Institute of San Francisco

THOMAS C. SCHELLING, John F. Kennedy School of Government, Harvard University

WOLFGANG SCHMIDT, Social Sciences Department, Alcoholism and Drug Addiction Research Foundation, Toronto

NORMAN SCOTCH, School of Public Health, and Department of Sociomedical Sciences and Community Medicine, School of Medicine, Boston University

DONALD J. TREIMAN, Department of Sociology, University of California, Los Angeles

JACQUELINE P. WISEMAN, Department of Sociology, University of California, San Diego

DEAN R. GERSTEIN, Study Director
ELAINE McGARRAUGH, Staff Associate
BEVERLY R. BLAKEY, Administrative Secretary

Preface

When the National Research Council report *Alcohol and Public Policy: Beyond the Shadow of Prohibition* was published in 1981, I felt that my colleagues on the project had done their work with signal dedication and grace, and thus our study of policy alternatives for the prevention of alcohol abuse and alcoholism would amply reward anyone's close attention. The managers of the National Institute on Alcohol Abuse and Alcoholism (NIAAA), the federal agency that commissioned the study, evidently concurred in this judgment. Shortly after publication of the report, at the request and sponsorship of NIAAA, we began to organize a follow-up conference to discuss the report's findings and recommendations.

The purpose of the conference was twofold. First, it was intended to generate wider public knowledge and discussion of *Alcohol and Public Policy* and to stimulate responses not only from researchers but also from practitioners well acquainted with both the competing values and priorities and the difficult administrative and political accommodations that must be reached to accomplish anything in this complex area. Second, we hoped the conference would be an opportunity to learn more about recent prevention efforts, especially local policy initiatives and opportunities for integrating voluntary, private, and governmental action. It is doubtless premature to expect scientific conclusions to be drawn about the effectiveness of new initiatives, but knowledge of them would benefit and encourage the large, fragmented audience interested in research and development of prevention efforts.

vii

The conference was designed and managed by a steering group chosen to reflect this agenda. Four of its members made contributions to the original report: political scientist Dan Beauchamp from the University of North Carolina, economist Philip Cook from Duke University, attorney-researcher James Mosher from the Medical Research Institute of San Francisco, and myself, a public policy analyst at the John F. Kennedy School of Government at Harvard. The eight other members brought to the task a remarkable range of experience: psychologist Howard Blane from the University of Pittsburgh and sociologist Robert Straus from the University of Kentucky are veteran researchers and policy advisers; Marilyn Goldwater of the Maryland General Assembly and Anne Lindeman of the Arizona Senate are experienced state legislators and health care professionals who have taken active roles in the National Conference of State Legislatures; Connecticut alcohol and drug abuse commissioner Donald McConnell is chair of the National Association of State Alcohol and Drug Abuse Directors; Frank Raflo is a Virginia businessman, publisher, county supervisor, and chairman of the mental health subcommittee of the National Association of Counties; Nebraska attorney John Doyle is chairman of the national board of directors of the National Council on Alcoholism; and Sheila Blume of New York is a psychiatrist, educator, former New York state alcohol division director, and national leader in the field of research and treatment for alcoholism.

The conference, held at the National Academy of Sciences on May 20 and 21, 1983, alternated between the perspectives of academic researchers and those of policy practitioners. The conference was itself something of a policy experiment in that it combined these groups to try to further their distinct but mutually regarding interests. It began with an overview of the prevention perspective and continued with sessions on selected topics from *Alcohol and Public Policy* that had sparked the most interest among members of the steering group and represented the broad angles of the report. There were sessions on regulating the supply of alcoholic beverages through taxes and defining the responsibilities of servers; modes of communication about alcohol, including mass communications and education of young people; and community cooperation to reduce alcohol problems by combining supply-based, educational, and other efforts at prevention in a variety of local and regional contexts.

In preparing this volume, we did not aim to systematically criticize or take issue with arguments expressed by the conferees. Our goal was rather to capture the incisive, informative character of the conference and make this record accessible and useful to readers. We have taken advantage of papers commissioned for each session, transcripts of the discussion, and revised comments and documents submitted afterward by conferees. All of the remarks here were reviewed by their makers at an early stage to ensure the faithful rendering of their ideas, and we have worked hard to maintain that faith while carrying out substantial editorial rearrangements, deletions, and textual amendments for the sake of clarity and continuity. The resulting volume is not a verbatim record of what took place on May 20 and 21, 1983, but it is in our view a unique colloquy of the major points of public policy with which *Alcohol and Public Policy* is concerned.

A central role in communicating with conferees and in gathering and overseeing materials for this volume belongs to National Research Council staff associate Elaine McGarraugh. We are also grateful for the invaluable assistance of Beverly Blakey, administrative secretary to the panel, and for the timely support offered by the staff of the National Research Council's Commission on Behavioral and Social Sciences and Education, the Office of Public Affairs, and the Meetings Office. Joan White, our project officer at NIAAA, has been thoughtful and supportive throughout this enterprise. We must acknowledge collectively the aid of over 100 individuals in more than 30 organizations who helped us identify the right people to appoint to the steering group and to invite to the conference. The support of the panel for the decision to extend our mandate to include the follow-up conference and this volume is deeply appreciated. The task has been enriched and eased by the talents of our study director and editor of this volume, Dean Gerstein.

The final and largest share of thanks must be reserved for the thoughtful, committed people who attended the conference and are represented in the pages that follow.

MARK H. MOORE, *Chair*
Panel on Alternative Policies Affecting
   the Prevention of Alcohol Abuse and
   Alcoholism

Contents

Toward the Prevention of Alcohol Problems

1 Introduction

The National Research Council accepted a difficult assignment five years ago in agreeing to organize an objective and comprehensive study of historical, current, and proposed programs and policies—many of them controversial—aimed at preventing alcohol abuse and alcoholism. The panel was asked by the National Institute on Alcohol Abuse and Alcoholism to:

• delineate the conceptual, normative, and political dimensions of the problem;

• find and evaluate the best available evidence concerning the effectiveness of preventive measures; and

• provide a clear set of conclusions to guide further research and debate on practical means to prevent or reduce alcohol-related problems.

The report we produced in 1981 was *Alcohol and Public Policy: Beyond the Shadow of Prohibition.* In it we presented a portrait of alcohol problems and possibilities for dealing with them that turned out to be slightly different from what most people had been thinking about before. We began with the idea that public policy in a democracy is a very subtle concept. People often imagine that it is located in the official documents of legislatures and the speeches of chief elected officials, or that it lies in the mechanics of programs. Our view was that public policy in a democracy is what people say, do, and believe.

1

CONCEPTUAL DIMENSIONS OF ALCOHOL PROBLEMS

When we looked at public policy on alcohol over the last generation in the United States, we noticed a certain coherence. Alcohol problems have been seen largely as the problems of alcoholics, and the most important way to deal with them has been to identify efficiently the people who are alcoholic and to treat them as effectively as possible. That was a sensible policy. It put on the table a very important piece of the alcohol problem, probably the largest single piece, and managed it in an interesting and valuable way. Voluntary organizations have been committed to that cause, and the approach has created considerable public awareness.

A Changing Conception of Alcohol Policy

At the same time, it seemed clear that many alcohol problems are caused by people who could in no useful sense be called alcoholics and who would rightfully be surprised to be counted in that group. While alcoholics have contributed the largest share of alcohol problems, noticeable pieces of the problem, conceived in its entirety, have been generated by ordinary people drinking recklessly, unwisely, or in conjunction with inappropriate activities. These people, standing at risk in ways they might not quite appreciate, stood out clearly in the aggregate statistics of fatalities, social disruption, and costs of health care. This piece of the alcohol problem was simply out of the reach of treatment instruments, and it seemed important not only for these individuals but also for society as a whole to find ways to deal with these problems effectively. It was this dimension that seemed to us out of focus in the existing strategy of treating alcoholism.

We thought it important, then, to examine public policy instruments that might successfully handle this piece of the problem. These instruments had to have some rather special characteristics: they had to operate across a very large segment of the population, and they had to rest lightly. They could not be controlling, containing, powerful instruments; they had to be broad, consistent, yet light in structuring incentives for the general population.

We suspected that policy instruments that would be effective in dealing with neglected alcohol problems and shaping drinking practices in the general population might also help reduce the rate at which people become alcoholic or advance to chronic or very dangerous levels of consumption. Such policy instruments might even help move current alcoholics out of their alcoholism by giving them added support in staying away from drinking. These possibilities, too, seemed somewhat peripheral to the current conception of alcoholism.

We scanned the possibilities for controlling these problems without overly constraining people's freedom of choice or preventing them from taking advantage of the benefits offered by alcohol.Our conclusion was that more attention needed to be given to the underemphasized area of prevention—not individualized approaches such as early detection and intervention, designed to reach hidden alcoholics or prealcoholics, but nonpersonalized approaches that would operate broadly on drinking practices throughout the population or break typical links between drinking practices and adverse consequences.

THREE ASPECTS OF PREVENTION

We divided the general concept of prevention into three somewhat narrower ideas. The first was to affect the terms and conditions under which alcohol is available, through special taxes, minimum age requirements, regulation of outlets and availability and times of sale—all the things that determine how easy and convenient it is for people to have access to alcohol. We imagined using the apparatus of distribution to affect not only how much people drink, but also conceivably when, where, and how they do their drinking. This seemed important, given our belief that many of the bad consequences of drinking were associated as much with when, where, and how people drink as with simply how much.

The second idea was to shape drinking practices directly by talking to people about what constitutes safe and appropriate drinking behavior. That could be done informally, through educational approaches (sponsored by the state or by others), as well as formally, through the special weight of laws instructing people on what constitutes safe and appropriate versus suspect or criminal practices. Such laws would invoke the prestige and coercive power of the state on behalf of these particular conceptions.

The third idea was to make the environment a safer one in which to be drunk. This idea included redesign of consumer products, rearrangement of places so that people might drink more safely in them, arranging transportation to get drinkers back home as safely as possible. We found this category interesting in that it included efforts to break the link between drinking and certain sets of consequences.

Given these three broad classes of prevention instruments, which we considered logically available, our next task was to find evidence on whether these approaches would work. For some, we found a modest amount of positive or negative evidence, while for others we could only state the logical possibilities since there was no evidence to demonstrate whether they could succeed.

We found the most evidence in the area of terms and conditions of supply. This persuaded us that raising taxes could have substantial effects on levels of alcohol use as well as on deaths from liver cirrhosis and traffic fatalities. There was also good evidence to show that adjusting the drinking age up or down has an effect on traffic fatalities. The other approaches, including teaching people to drink safely and well through education or the law and making the world somewhat safer for intoxication, were less well backed by empirical evidence, but stood as opportunities for society to consider and experiment with.

In short, when we reviewed the evidence and the logic of the problem, some specifics within the three broad areas seemed possible or likely to be effective. That became our conclusion. It did not claim a great deal, but what it did claim was important, and it implied that the nation's strategy should shift enough to build up more kinds of prevention-oriented approaches to alcohol problems.

FOCUSING ON PREVENTION EFFORTS

Two major developments occurred between the last meeting of the panel that authored *Alcohol and Public Policy,* in May 1980, and the follow-up conference from which the present report derives, in May 1983. The first development began with the national election of 1980: in its aftermath a series of policy changes substantially affected relations between the federal and the state governments, markedly altering the role of the National Institute on Alcohol Abuse and Alcoholism (NIAAA) in activities at the state level. These changes, particularly the absorption of many state-administered federal programs into the block grant system, moved a great deal of detailed programmatic decision making out of the federal agency and into the statehouses.

The second development was the remarkable growth of citizen and legislative concern with the problem of drunk driving, spurred by the formation of grass-roots organizations such as Mothers Against Drunk Drivers (MADD), Remove Intoxicated Drivers (RID), and Students Against Drunk Driving (SADD). Working on the county and state levels, these groups spearheaded movements to raise the drinking age, and also turned their efforts toward more assured use of criminal penalties and civil liability actions, adoption of alcohol-education curricula by school boards, increasing police attention, surveillance of courtroom actions, and other related issues.

The concatenation of these events argued for focusing our follow-up effort at least in part on state and local prevention opportunities, a focus not difficult to reconcile with the report, since virtually all the options it discussed were subject to implementation at these levels.

ORGANIZATION OF THE VOLUME

Of course it would have been impossible for this or any other conference to be comprehensive in examining local and regional prevention efforts, nor would that have served the purpose of generating discussion based on the 1981 report. We chose instead to draw a matched sample: first, a handful of the most prominent and interesting policy instruments discussed in the report, selected to represent the three broad classes of instruments as well as different degrees of experience with implementation; second, a selection of individuals from across the country and across the landscape of viewpoints and activities involving prevention and alcohol policy. A number of the conferees were asked to prepare remarks beforehand in the form of brief papers or essays. These pieces served to open discussion of each prevention instrument; thereafter, the conferees took each subject through its own paces in spirited and candid discourse. Each chapter in this volume includes one or more papers or essays, followed by discussions edited from the conference transcripts.

Chapter 2 sounds the general theme around which the conference turned: the idea of community ownership of alcohol problems. This idea is simple yet elusive. It means collectively owning up to the problem—acknowledging that it belongs to every individual who is part of the community and accepting responsibility for carrying out solutions—which may entail a measure of sacrifice, in one form or another, for everyone. In this context, William Mayer, then administrator of the federal Alcohol, Drug Abuse, and Mental Health Administration (ADAMHA), compares alcohol abuse to the great public health challenges of the past, calling on Americans to mobilize and act in concert to further our traditional public health ideals. Illinois mental health commissioner Margaret Hastings reminds us that calls for community action are inherently competitive with other agendas; she notes the political obstacles that prevention interests must overcome, as well as the political assets they can wield. Frank Raflo, supervisor of Loudoun County, Virginia, then draws us directly into the thinking of key community members, poignantly illustrating the common sensibility that recognizes alcohol problems as serious—but as belonging to someone else. Chapter 2 concludes with an exchange between research scholar

Mark Keller and conference chair Mark Moore on whether our institutions and leaders bear a collective responsibility to take preventive action with the various instruments now at hand, or whether we should forgo such action and await future generations whose attitudes toward drinking may be revised by an educational process that we can only initiate.

Chapters 3 through 6 examine in greater detail a sample of policy options in the areas of regulating the supply of alcohol and shaping drinking practices directly. Chapter 3, beginning with a summary by economist Philip Cook, focuses on the ways in which alcohol—its consumption, distribution, and abuse—affects and is affected by the taxing and spending powers of legislatures. This chapter handles two controversial themes: the strategic importance of alcohol taxes as both a potential preventive measure per se and a potential source of funds for general revenue and preventive programs; and the tactical dimension, in which political coalitions form around diverse interests—economic, health, and criminal justice—touched by tax issues.

Chapter 4 examines the responsibilities of businesses, both as suppliers who may be subject to liability for their product's abuse and who can take steps to prevent or curtail such abuse, and as employers concerned with the performance and welfare of their work force. Beginning with attorney-researcher James Mosher's paper on comprehensive server intervention, this chapter notes the role of legal and regulatory actions as well as voluntary initiatives by beverage servers and other firms and describes a number of joint public-private ventures in this field.

Chapter 5 comes to grips with the mass media, particularly the role of television programming and advertising in creating images and conveying information about alcohol use and its consequences. After reviewing the major scientific studies that bear on the relation of mass media to alcohol abuse, health educator Lawrence Wallack, in his lead paper, concludes that ethical values and logical principles must remain the major guides to coordinating action in this realm. The conferees take up this challenge, painting a broad spectrum of such guides.

Chapter 6 concerns drinking and drunk driving among young people, two highly charged aspects of alcohol abuse that have become firmly linked in public debate and policy, although, as the discussion indicates, each problem extends beyond that direct linkage. The lead essay on parental action is by Keith Schuchard, research director of the Parental Resource Institute for Drug Education (PRIDE).

Chapter 7 draws together most of the main themes of the conference, following a lead essay by Robert Reynolds, San Diego County Alcohol

Program chief. It brings into focus the third major area of prevention instruments, those that modify the environment to reduce risk. This final chapter concentrates on the community level, where all preventive policies must take effect or at least draw on grass-roots support to be politically viable. It concludes, in counterpoint to where the panel began, with questions about the detailed shape and scope of the problems and the effectiveness of alternative preventive programs in local communities. State and county policy makers strongly encourage NIAAA to extend its work in bringing this sort of information into their hands.

RECURRENT THEMES

The conferees do not seek or reach any grand consensus that could form a ringing conclusion to these proceedings. Their periodic return during the discussions to the most general issues shows that it is difficult enough just to grasp fully the broad prevention strategy recommended in *Alcohol and Public Policy*. Although presented as a fairly simple idea, this strategy runs askew from nearly everything we have been thinking about alcohol problems for many years; we are all to some degree prisoners of persistent habits of thought, the power of which we only dimly perceive. Prevention still seems automatically to suggest particular instruments—selective prohibition, efforts aimed at youth, or punitive laws. While none of these ideas is completely out of line, each represents only a single, limited set of possibilities that, if stretched too far, becomes ineffective, untenable, or destructive. The broader idea of prevention encompasses dozens of creative, well-balanced possibilities linked by the simple prescription that they be general, non-personalized, and dedicated to reducing the aggregate risk of harmful consequences.

IMPORTANT ISSUES IN ALCOHOL POLICY

This conference also brings home the point that there is no simple structure for implementing the general idea of prevention. Legislators, executive branch officials, treatment providers, and business and volunteer group leaders keep using such words as "networking," "organizing," and "politicking," because there is no central bureaucratic site to approach, no single structure within which to carry out many of these prevention policies. The capacity to act is dispersed broadly throughout society; therefore, to mobilize it, to start the body politic marching in a particular direction, one has to network, organize, and politick.

This is no less true of alcohol policy as it currently exists. No one simply announced that as of 1960 or 1975 our alcohol policy was to treat alcoholics. What organized this policy was a series of shared perceptions about what the problem was and what people were trying to do. It is hard to grasp a revised strategy and even harder to develop a structure or consensus for it, but clearly there are three operating levels on which such things are ultimately worked out: politics, policies, and programs.

POLITICS, POLICIES, AND PROGRAMS

By politics, we mean the Aristotelian idea of trying to change people's minds about what a problem is and what can reasonably be done about it. To a certain extent, *Alcohol and Public Policy* is a part of politics: it has become a common discussion item, a touchstone that people can use to certify the legitimacy and complementarity of a broad band of possible preventive measures. Discussing, arguing, and thinking about which values are to be served and which subordinated in particular situations, and trying to agree on what the world is really like, are what democratic republican politics means. Our report seems to have earned a place in that tradition.

The second operating level is policies. It is important to understand that many of the things discussed here involve little government money. They use another very productive resource of the state: authority backed by moral leadership. This formulation may sound old-fashioned, but the state in fact produces many effects simply by leading, by using its authority and its moral position, as well as by taxing and spending. Measures such as liability and the educational impact of laws work without spending vast amounts of government money. They work rather by reminding people of their responsibilities to the community.

Finally, there is the level of programs. This is where bureaucracies spend money and volunteer groups design and carry out particular ideas. Many people think the core of the issue has not been reached until one starts to talk about programs. But something is accomplished even when we talk only about politics and policies. When we are politicking, not only are we building support for policies and programs, but very often we also go much of the way toward implementing them. When people are persuaded to attend to a certain piece of the alcohol problem and begin acting on it, the result is often strong volunteer efforts. This volume describes such efforts by the Caucus of Producers, Writers, and Directors; Mothers Against Drunk Drivers; the Georgia Power Company; and many others. Much of this work goes on without direct government sponsorship. Encouragement that comes from knowledge and the redefinition of problems, and the energy that we always associate with voluntary initiative can augment or exceed the programmatic, bureaucratic, funding-based capability of the government.

PREVENTION POLICIES AND THE ALCOHOL BEVERAGE INDUSTRY

One prominent issue in this field is the relationship between proposals for prevention policies and the position of the alcohol beverage industry. There is a strong temptation to see these interests as inevitably and diametrically opposed, to think that when prevention policies gain force, the alcohol beverage industry has to take losses. There may be hard truth to this view. All prevention policies, to be successful, may have to slice into the business of the beverage-making and beverage-serving industry, and it seems reasonable for those in the industry to be concerned.

At the same time, it is important to take account of a possibility that may seem remote or utopian: that the alcohol beverage industry, those who produce, market, and sell the products, may have a propitious opportunity to make a contribution. The practices and proposals of the S & A Restaurant Corporation, for example, or the advertising restrictions that members of Wine Institute have imposed on themselves, ought to please anyone interested in prevention approaches. It would be a mistake to look down on such efforts, to abandon them, or to think that they were ultimately irrelevant. The public commitment, knowledge, and position of the alcohol beverage industry could have real potential for helping to prevent harmful consequences of alcohol use while protecting as much appropriate use as society can manage. We cannot know for certain at this stage exactly how much potential to reduce problems might have to be sacrificed to avoid cutting too far into appropriate drinking. There may be a very harsh trade-off, and it may be very optimistic to think that one could solve many problems without cutting deeply into consumption. Whatever the particulars, it is clear that we face a very complicated social decision on how much loss to take in legitimate consumption for how much gain in reducing problems associated with alcohol use.

CONCLUSION

It expresses the final and overall sense of the conference to say that, as we move further into prevention, there should be as much sharing of responsibility and cooperative enterprise as possible. It is crucial to take advantage of the wide body of experimentation now going on throughout the country and to learn as much as possible from the variety of approaches to prevention, ranging from taxation, to controls over availability, to educational enterprises through private or governmental groups, to making the world safer to drink in. It is highly appropriate for the National Institute on Alcohol Abuse and Alcoholism to support and serve as a conduit of high-quality information about the success—and failure, when that occurs—of these experiments in prevention policy.

2 Prevention and the Community

PUBLIC HEALTH IDEALS AND NATIONAL OBJECTIVES

WILLIAM MAYER, Alcohol, Drug Abuse, and Mental Health Administration

The easy problems in public health have mainly been solved.

Alcohol-related problems are far more complicated and their solutions more fraught with trouble than when our predecessors tried to clean up the water supply, wipe out cholera and dysentery, and immunize people against smallpox. I do not mean to suggest that conquering smallpox and purifying the water supply were really easy. Riots were connected with the idea of inoculating innocent babies with scrapings from diseased cows. But we see in alcohol-related problems a spectrum of considerations broader than any involved in the great achievements of public health in the past.

Attempts to solve problems of *alcoholism* have not been sufficient to address the broader public health issues involved in *alcohol consumption*. As Moore and Gerstein (1981:44) point out: "While chronic drinkers with high consumption both cause and suffer far more than their numerical share of adverse consequences of drinking, their share of alcohol problems is still only a fraction—typically less than half—of the total. Alcohol problems occur throughout the drinking population; they occur at lower rates but among much greater numbers as one moves from the heaviest drinkers to more moderate drinkers." Since many health and social problems related to the use of alcohol clearly

11

lie far beyond the range of treatment and prevention services that we can offer to the individual, some approaches to prevention are inextricably tied up with matters of pressing and important public policy.

The National Institute on Alcohol Abuse and Alcoholism (NIAAA) is mandated to support a broad base of informative studies that can be used in the search for effective measures to prevent alcohol-related problems. That is why we asked the National Academy of Sciences to convene this remarkably diverse collection of people—including state, national, and local policy makers and lawmakers, researchers, professional people, treatment providers, civic leaders, and economic leaders—to try to examine together from each special point of view (and no field has more special points of view than that of alcohol abuse and alcoholism) the implications and possible applications of the National Research Council report. This conference is a nucleus for the kind of a broad general debate that will help to determine public policy for preventing alcohol-related problems.

Some issues raised by the report are highly controversial, not just in this country but around the world. Among the most controversial prevention policies identified in the report are ones that influence the pricing, taxing, and availability of alcohol. Less controversial, perhaps, are policies for shaping drinking practices through education (though it is unclear how effectively we can do that), public information and training programs, and laws regarding drinking and driving and public drunkenness. Finally, there are policies to promote environmental safety for drinkers and others in the workplace, in the home, in public recreational areas, on the streets, and on the highways.

The three kinds of approaches specified in the report conform in an interesting way to the traditional categories of solutions to major public health problems. The first approach, having to do with the supply of alcoholic beverages, conforms in a sense to the public health focus on the causative agent and its vectors. Second, shaping the drinking practices of individuals and groups resembles closely the public health preoccupation with the host who accepts the agent. Third, attention to manipulating the environment is a fundamental underpinning to many great achievements of public health in the past.

The report offered recommendations for research and policy discussion in each of these areas. We hope to stimulate lively and spirited discussion, both pro and con, of the report's recommendations and to encourage further high-quality research in this complex field.

This is a particularly opportune time for such discussions to take place. It is clear to those who have worked for any length of time in this field that the extent and quality of attention now being directed toward alcohol-related problems is without precedent in our lifetimes. States, local areas, and the private sector at all levels are giving attention in new ways to alcohol-related problems that have had such debilitating effects on our society, effects that have for so long been denied. Alcohol abuse and alcoholism are now being recognized here and throughout the world as major public health problems, and prevention has a high priority in this administration. Examples include the Presidential Commission on Drunk Driving, the Department of Health and Human Services' Secretarial Initiative on teenage alcohol abuse, and the enormous relative increases in the 1983 and 1984 federal research budget for alcohol abuse and alcoholism, which far outstripped increases for research in other health areas.

This is a time for everyone to contribute to the solution of problems far too long ignored. Progress has been impeded by the special biases, however sincere, held by various elements who have been at war with one another for the last 10 years over the best way to approach alcohol problems. Almost none of us is innocent of participation in such battles. What is abundantly clear in the National Research Council report is the need for many disciplines, many social agents, and agencies with quite different agendas to become involved, to draw together, to communicate freely and openly with one another, and thus to avoid the dangers of simplistic and retributive measures, and of simply defending special biases.

In short, we should join our efforts together as Americans traditionally have when faced with great national problems, to reverse a dangerous, fatal, devastating social and health problem that we can only hope to solve collectively, as a people.

POLITICAL REALITIES AT THE STATEHOUSE

MARGARET HASTINGS, Illinois Commission on Mental Health and Developmental Disabilities

Prevention is a public health ideal that everyone favors—in the abstract. But when it comes to voting on real programs and real dollars, prevention policy has certain politically difficult characteristics.

First, prevention is futuristic. It requires a commitment to future outcomes, not short-term results. This is antithetical to an American political need attached to short electoral cycles: the need to show immediate gains. Elected officials have a hard time voting for prevention programs unless there is a well-educated constituency willing to keep those programs alive by reelecting leaders who support future-oriented policies.

Second, state and national legislation in this country is usually fostered by advocacy groups concerned with specific categorical problems, such as blindness or heart disease. Prevention cuts across categories. It is a comprehensive concept, not a casualty area. This absence of a specific constituency can act as an obstacle politically. Although prevention efforts may be seen as humane and cost-effective, they have trouble moving to the forefront of national, state, and local health and human services policy. The lack of a constituency often makes prevention programs most vulnerable to funding cuts.

Third, because good prevention programming cuts across many categories, coordination becomes essential between agencies, within communities, and among professionals, volunteers, and citizen leaders. This requires an unusual willingness to set priorities, share responsibilities, and believe in causes beyond a single individual, agency, or organizational turf.

Fourth, prevention policy has an impact on personal value systems. Prevention programs may demand greater personal responsibility and challenge life-style choices and excessive personal freedom. In my seven years of experience in developing state policy, the potential collision of values has been the major hurdle, and it grows more complicated as our belief systems become more pluralistic. Enormous pressures on legislators from individual industries, religions, and special interest groups make consensus difficult. These pressure groups often have far more influence on policy than their actual number of supporters would suggest. When a collision in values occurs, it must be resolved through a new consensus on a purpose more general than the individual interests of the groups involved.

Recent efforts to restrict drunk driving and smoking in public places, for example, show that we are collectively beginning to endorse limited regulation of life-style—but primarily in areas in which self-destructive behavior also affects others. We have known for years, for example, that young drunk drivers were killing themselves. But not until the relatives of victims of drunk drivers organized did we begin to change laws and policies. These new, articulate constituencies have changed attitudes and reshaped public opinion, a necessary precursor to policy changes.

A second area in which life-style choices affect others is health care costs. The state of Illinois, for example, supports hundreds of nursing home residents who have drunk so much for so long that they are nonfunctional and brain-damaged, with serious sensory and cognitive deficits. No one was too concerned about this expense before this era of finite resources. Now we have to allocate scarce public dollars among many needy populations. The second-largest expense in many state governments is Medicaid, and much of that cost is alcohol-related. About 40-60 percent of all hospitalizations are alcohol-related. Alcohol is involved in high percentages of reported child abuse incidents, suicides, assaults, and homicides. These events, plus accidents, represent a major national expense in illness care and lost productivity. Recent studies show that life-style factors account for as much as half of illness costs, which now total more than 10 percent of the nation's gross national product. These findings provide new political impetus for prevention policies.

We have found in Illinois that state prevention planning can be thought of in terms of three areas: services (particularly for high-risk groups), regulation, and education. The state has set out to develop a prevention plan for alcoholism that brings all the relevant groups together. We selected priorities within each area, considered where we could intervene to have an impact on the priorities, and defined the appropriations and the responsibility for policies so that each priority could have a sufficiently broad-based constituency. We have had a difficult time agreeing which prevention programs should have priority, due to difficulties in measuring relative cost-effectiveness. Again and again an isolated agency would get an idea and develop it, but the system would not sustain it long enough for claims of long-term results to be substantiated. People involved in the budgetary process would say, "We want to give money to treatment instead, because that is the only thing that we *know* works." There has to be firm priority setting, and there has to be ownership of issues by key legislators so that monies and ideas will remain intact when various special interest groups attack them.

One of our most successful prevention efforts in Illinois used block grant money to establish two prevention resource centers, which were repositories of information, materials, and people who were highly skilled in how to set up local prevention programs. The centers were available free of charge to community groups to help them develop their own prevention programs. Budgets for prevention programs are protected most effectively when there is community ownership of the idea—not just the schools or a parent group, but a consortium of community institutions. Then the chances that the prevention program will last are great. If programs are limited to the schools, the possibility of their having lasting impact in the community is small. Effective prevention policy depends on developing efforts in a variety of areas simultaneously, with effective follow-up and evaluation efforts built into programs and with a broad base of community involvement and support that can keep elected officials committed to prevention.

COMMUNITY MOVERS AND SHAKERS

FRANK RAFLO, County of Loudoun, Virginia

In order to talk about community support, community involvement, community ownership, and the like, we need to know what a community is. Is it people, a place, organizations, a series of stores located on the same block, an area that has its own radio station or newspaper? Obviously, all of those elements might fit the definition of a community. Who, then, are the community movers and shakers we must look to in trying to prevent problems associated with alcohol?

I want to introduce you to a few of them. Each one represents an important sector of what we identify as a community. I hope that after you have met them you will have a better conception of what goes into community action.

One common thread will become clear. They all recognize alcohol as a "community problem" and express a willingness, indeed a strong motivation, to do something about it. At the same time, in identifying alcohol as a community problem, they certainly do not acknowledge it as belonging to them personally.

Here are my characters; their monologue may be a bit disjointed, but that is the character of everyday thought.

My name is Billy. I understand you want my advice about alcohol and drinking, and I am glad to give it to you.

I know it's a problem. I see some of the dudes almost every night bouncing around from joint to joint, old ones as well as young ones. The other morning, for instance, I stopped at the Seven-Eleven for a pack of smokes, and some of the local big shots were lined up outside the state liquor store waiting to be first in line for the 10 o'clock opening. And a little thing I found out when I worked for a while as a bellhop is that they're always brushing their teeth. There was one guy who would take a snort and right away head for the men's room to brush. His toothpaste and mouthwash bill was probably as high as his booze bill.

But I guess you really want to know what guys like me and our girls do. Simple: we cruise. Once in a while my girl and I split a beer or two at school—out on the back lot. But mostly it's weekend cruising: get in the car, load up with some six-packs and cruise. How old am I? Not

*old enough to buy the stuff, but there are plenty of guys out there who
will make the buy; after all, what's wrong with a few beers? It's better
than getting hooked on the other stuff.*

*Of course, there was the case of Harold. Two weeks ago he had a
couple too many and rammed into a telephone pole. We all went to the
funeral. It was too bad; he was a nice guy. He knew how to snag a pass
and was going to be a regular on the team next year. He should have
known better. I guess we should have warned him that you have to be
careful, you can't overdo it.*

*But as I was saying. We all work together here in this community:
buy for each other, drive for each other, cruise around with each other,
and get upset when someone has too much and flips over. You might
say we have a sense of community that recognizes that too much alcohol
is not good. But like our folks tell us, "Thank God it's only beer and
not dope."*

It is lunch time at the best restaurant in town. J.P., chief loan officer
at the bank and currently serving as public affairs chairman of the local
chamber of commerce, has just been seated with his friend, Henry
Bryant, assistant principal at the local high school.

*Henry, old boy, I do appreciate your coming. I know how busy you
are at school, trying to get those SAT scores up and keep a winning
football team at the same time—and doing a fine job. From what I
hear, you're in line for promotion to the top. The superintendent is a
good friend of mine; I've talked to him about you.*

*Oh waiter, bring me a bourbon and water. What will you have, Henry?
You want to pass? I guess that does look better; you don't want to smell
up the principal's office, do you?*

*I guess you're wondering why I asked you to come here today. It's
like this: I got stuck with the public affairs committee this year, and the
president and directors of the bank expect me to get some good community projects going—you know the kind, a community project that
will reflect well on the bank. It makes the directors feel good to read in
the local paper that one of their top executives is hanging in there with
a full load of community service. As I got to thinking about it, especially
after reading about that triple fatality last week, where the driver of
each of the cars was found to be loaded, I decided that the community
issue that should get top priority is alcohol.*

*So I asked myself, "How can we get this community involved in a
combined effort to combat and reduce alcoholism?" The answer was
obvious: Start with the youngsters. Education is our greatest asset, so*

let's use it. I know you agree, Henry, and that's where you come in. I've sent off to some of these national organizations, and now I have all of this printed material plus a couple of videotapes about drinking and the problems of alcohol, and the various ways a community can line up behind its schools and churches to bring this problem under control. And that's where you come in, Henry. I want you to set up a school assembly program for me—I'll do it at your convenience, just give me a week's notice. I'll notify Charley down at the newspaper to make sure he covers it. It will make a great picture, and I want you in it along with a couple of top athletes and maybe two or three of your best-looking cheerleaders—wearing their uniforms, of course.

Waiter, how about a short refill—just a sweetener to finish out my lunch.

So you check out the details, Henry, and if you have any trouble, just let me know. We're going to start with the school kids and plaster this town with educational information about the need for the community to get behind a program to tackle the problem of alcohol. I really don't understand it myself; I guess some people just don't know when they've had enough. They really ought to be ashamed of themselves.

You have to leave now? Thanks for listening. I hope you enjoyed lunch, and we'll be in touch.

My name is Sally. I'm married to Bill, I have two small kids and a pretty good life. He works and I stay home and mind the kids and do the chores. The kids are asleep, taking their nap, and I'm finishing up a bit of dusting. It's 3:15 in the afternoon—oops, there goes the phone.

Oh hello, Bill. You'll be late tonight? Yes, I'll go ahead without you and feed the children. Try to get back before they go to bed, dear. Sure, it's okay, no problem; your job comes first.

Oh damn, another evening with no one to talk to and nothing to do but watch that blasted television. I wish it were five o'clock; I sure could use my daily gin and tonic. I know you're not supposed to drink before five; they say it's a bad habit. But then, the kids are asleep, and there isn't going to be much peace and quiet around here when they get up, especially if Bill isn't here. I think I'll mix a short one. I won't make a habit of it. Just today, because he's not coming home for dinner.

Now that's more like it. There's nothing more relaxing than a gin and tonic, along with the peace and quiet of the afternoon. Maybe I'll have just a teenie refill later.

I have other friends in the community, and you may have a chance to meet them another time. But those you have met here are representative of my town. They are all concerned; you heard them say so themselves. They want to help. If you called them up to ask them to serve on a committee to study the problem of alcohol, I am sure each one would agree to serve. But be sure you don't get them too close to the real problem. After all, they really feel that, conceptually, drinking too much alcohol is shameful.

They are not the whole community. As in every community, we have a mix, and there are others who balance the wheel: those who work with the scouts, run the little league, provide other active recreation, sponsor book clubs, counsel at churches, teach in homes, and set examples of success without alcohol. We even have some in our community who teach kids how to say no when offered a drink. I may have picked out the wrong ones for you to meet, but they were the ones I could round up on short notice, and they are the ones you have to reach if you want to get the community involved in preventing alcohol abuse.

COMMENTS ON PREVENTION APPROACHES

MARK MOORE, Harvard University

Frank Raflo has put his finger on a central, bedeviling issue: who is a problem drinker, and who is not? We are used to thinking that anyone who drinks and is having associated problems such as unemployment or social or medical problems is an alcoholic, a "protoalcoholic," or a "near-alcoholic." Partly for that reason, anyone in the general population who gets drunk and is arrested or falls down stairs feels nervous about defining himself or herself as a "problem drinker," because that means that he or she is an alcoholic or is destined to become one, with all the associated special misery and special treatment.

Therefore, our panel, in writing *Alcohol and Public Policy*, tried to keep separate the concepts of "heavy drinking" and "problems associated with drinking." One result was to highlight occasional, ill-timed drunkenness. The problem of people getting drunk somewhat too often, perhaps in the wrong place or at the wrong time, exists alongside the problem of people getting drunk repetitively over a long enough period of time that they begin failing systematically across a broad range of their activities.

Just as when we look over time at the welfare population, the criminal-offending population, or panel surveys of drug abusers, we find that a small fraction of people stay in the worst condition, at the most deviant and extreme end, for a long time, and a great many people move back and forth at the nearer end. Some get into trouble while drinking at an early stage and their troubles keep getting worse; they seem to fit the traditional idea of alcoholism. Many others enter and leave periods of harmful drinking practices on their own more or less frequently. People are distributed all along the set of possibilities. The main problem, against which preventive policy instruments could be uniquely effective, is not so much the people who move rapidly to the far end of the distribution (for them we know that the best possible response is treatment of various types), but the people who move into and out of periods of harmful drinking practices intermittently, for a week or two, even a day or two, perhaps once every few months or years.

The interesting surprise the panel found is that the problem of ill-timed drunkenness, badly fit into the environment, generates a substantial portion of the medical problems, the violence and crime problems, the employment problems, and even the marital problems that involve alcohol. In other words, a large portion of the alcohol problem is created by people who would never think of themselves as problem drinkers.

As I watched Frank Raflo's characters materialize before us, each one drinking within, or at least not way outside, a normative pattern, I realized that these people were at risk. Partly the risk is that they might go on to higher levels of consumption, but presumably we are all at that risk all the time, and we all understand that if you move to very high levels of consumption, you can get into deep trouble. But they were also at risk in the moments that were described: The banker could have left the luncheon and made a mistake in his job; the housewife could have been inattentive to her child; Billy, cruising on the weekend, could get into an accident. Now, for any one of those individuals that risk is small, but from the community perspective, small probabilities distributed across big populations add up to big problems. The normative drinking patterns that Frank Raflo so graphically illustrated for us contain within them the possibilities for creating a big problem.

To attack this effectively, we have to emphasize policy instruments that cover large numbers of people—but uniformly and gently. Almost any device we could imagine that requires tailoring to individuals would be overwhelmingly expensive to apply to 50 million people.

MARK KELLER, Rutgers University

I want to raise a broad question about the effectiveness of generalized policy options, such as taxes on alcohol and restrictions on advertising for alcoholic beverages.

I am skeptical that increased taxation or substantially raising the price of alcohol can really affect the volume of alcohol consumption. A few years ago when I was in Russia, the price of vodka was about equivalent to $10 per liter here. The Russians cope with the high price in two ways. First, the very prosperous classes buy vodka at that price and drink much more of it than is good for them. Those who cannot afford the price, the working people, buy vodka on the black market, which supplies nearly as much as the government stores do, at a much better price. If the price of vodka were lower in Russia, would the Russians drink even more than they do now? That is really hard to imagine; I do not know if they could. So how important is the question of price?

My second example is advertising. Does advertising affect the volume of drinking? In Russia there has not been one advertisement for liquor in over 60 years. You do not have to advertise alcohol to people. Why is the industry here spending millions of dollars on advertising? Because there is competition over who is going to sell how much of what. But I do not know whether advertising really increases the volume of consumption.

MARK MOORE, Harvard University

Dr. Keller, I would quickly agree that we cannot specify how the major factors determine the level of alcohol consumption, nor are we clear about the relationship between any given level of consumption and a set of bad consequences associated with drinking. Many factors enter the set of equations that relate social conditions, individual drinking, and social consequences. You have discarded some of them; you argue that price is unimportant, as is the special influence of mass media, as contrasted with the power of family or ethnic traditions. So how can we possibly affect consumption or the links between consumption and harmful consequences? I hold no singular brief for shrinking consumption; what I want to do is shrink the problem. If that can be done in some way without affecting the volume of consumption, that is fine; if it cannot, then we have to decide how much we need to or are willing to reduce consumption to get the benefit of shrinking the problem. How can we intervene to reduce the total amount of alcohol problems now, with or without reducing consumption? Do you spot an opportunity, with your many years of experience in this area?

MARK KELLER, Rutgers University

I think education is very important. It is different from advertising, which has a different purpose. I believe that a real reduction of alcohol problems has to come from a change in the attitude that people have toward drinking, toward what you drink, how much you drink, when you drink, and so forth. People have a complicated involvement with alcohol, all of which needs to be changed if we are going to reduce the problems. I believe that it can work through a variety of educational methods, and that it will be a long, generational process. I think we can significantly reduce alcohol problems in this country in about 200-300 years. I would not be discouraged in trying for that, because it is the only thing that will work, in my opinion.

MARK MOORE, Harvard University

I think you would find a high degree of agreement that the fundamental issue is to change cultural attitudes about what constitutes appropriate, normative drinking practices in society. In general we would like to shape that set of norms so as to end up with fewer drinking problems— not zero drinking, not unlimited drinking, but some level of drinking with a much lower profile of harmful consequences than we now experience.

When we try to think concretely about how to affect people's attitudes, we think of using many things that are available to us, not only education programs, but also taxes and hours of sale that make buying less convenient. People's dietary habits changed some years ago, partly when they discovered that too much red meat was bad for them, and partly when the price of red meat doubled. Those two things went hand in hand. All our knowledge about how people's attitudes change suggests that they often go hand in hand. Again, in the late 1960s, when cigarette advertising was still on television, antismoking commercials appeared as the result of a lawsuit brought by John Banzhaf. At the same time, many states increased their cigarette taxes. Overall, average smoking rates fell in that period. Often there is some real condition that changes in the world, and then behavior changes; attitudes tend to follow along and become consolidated behind the new set of conditions. Much of what we are talking about here involves exactly the process you described. It is just that we see no particular reason to restrict efforts to an instrument called education, which typically means special classes in elementary schools.

MARK KELLER, Rutgers University

I think we can be much broader than that about education. Let me say something about the effect of prices. I do not believe that Americans are strongly affected by prices. I do not believe Americans cut down on red meat because the price went up. At the same time that the price of the meat went up, the price of fish went up even more, yet they are buying more fish.

MARK MOORE, Harvard University

The price of fish went up as demand shifted. But let me give you one more example. Another major social innovation was the reduction in traffic fatalities that occurred after the 55 mph speed limit became law. Again, the lower speed limit was passed at the same time that the price of oil was rapidly increasing. We think we cannot effect small changes in behavior via price shifts, mass media, and the like. And yet the smoking example, the dietary example, and the driving example all provide concrete evidence that our society does, in relatively short periods, have the capacity to alter people's conduct, at least a little in some areas that may not mean that much to them. Now you could say, "The difficulty here is that alcohol means an awful lot to them." I don't know. Maybe you are right, maybe you are wrong—maybe we should find out.

3 Taxing and Spending

INCREASING THE FEDERAL ALCOHOL EXCISE TAX

PHILIP J. COOK, Duke University

Inflation and the Erosion of the Excise Tax

The prices of alcoholic beverages have been declining rapidly in recent years in comparison with prices of other consumer items. Consumer price index statistics indicate that since 1967 the real price of all alcoholic beverages has declined 27 percent. Distilled spirits have led the way with a 48 percent fall in price, followed by beer (25 percent) and wine (19 percent). The results of econometric and epidemiologic studies show that such reductions in relative price have the effect of promoting alcohol consumption and increasing the incidence of alcohol-related problems.

The fact that liquor prices are currently at about one-half of the 1967 level can be attributed in part to congressional inaction with respect to federal excise taxes on alcoholic beverages. Current federal excise tax rates were set in 1951 but have been largely repealed by inflation since then. If the federal tax had been indexed to the consumer price index in 1967, the cost of a fifth of liquor would currently be about $3.50 higher. Indexing the beer tax would have had a smaller but still substantial effect on beer prices. It can be argued that the failure of Congress to increase taxes in step with inflation constitutes the most impor-

24

tant feature of federal government policy in alcohol abuse prevention during the past 15 years.

The recent wave of concern over mounting federal deficits has put the federal alcohol tax back on the national political agenda. There is an obvious parallel with the federal cigarette tax, which had also been left at its Korean War level—$.08 per pack—for 30 years and then was doubled by Congress in 1982. While the impetus for raising this tax was a concern with "revenue enhancement," the more important consequence will be to promote the public health by reducing smoking. Similarly, an important consequence of an increase in the alcohol tax would be to reduce alcohol abuse and its attendant personal and social costs. I summarize here the evidence on the preventive effects of alcohol taxes and then discuss the distributional and revenue impacts of a tax increase.

Alcohol Taxes and the Rate of Alcohol Abuse

Alcohol abuse is a major public health problem. There are roughly 75,000 alcohol-related deaths each year (Gerstein, 1981:205). Chronic heavy drinking is responsible for a large fraction of the more than 27,000 deaths each year due to liver cirrhosis as well as about 5,000 deaths classified as resulting from "alcoholism." The remaining alcohol-related deaths involve failures in judgment, attention, and physical coordination resulting from inebriation, including about 25,000 alcohol-related auto fatalities and a number of other accidents, homicides, and suicides. Alcohol-related morbidity and injuries impose a considerable burden on the health care system. A recent estimate (Schifrin, 1983) of health care costs stemming from alcohol-related problems is $20 billion for 1979—about 10 percent of total health care expenditures for that year. The cost of absenteeism and reduced productivity associated with employee drinking and premature death is even greater—roughly $78 billion in 1979 (Schifrin, 1983).

For alcohol taxes to be an effective policy instrument for reducing these and other costs associated with alcohol abuse, it must be true that higher alcohol prices reduce the prevalence of chronic heavy drinking and the incidence of drunkenness. An increase in taxes on liquor, wine, or beer results in an increase in the average prices of these commodities and a reduction in alcohol consumption from these sources. (More precisely, consumption is less than it would have been without the tax increase.) This result has been established quite conclusively for data from the United States and Canada (Johnson and Okanen, 1977; Ornstein and Hanssens, 1981; Cook and Tauchen, 1982). More important and controversial is the question of how taxes and prices influence the consumption levels of the heaviest drinkers. It is logically possible that average consumption would fall as a result of a tax increase solely due to its effect on moderate drinkers; the heaviest drinkers are immune to economic incentives. An argument supporting this possibility can be stated by a chain of propositions: (1) a large portion of the heaviest drinkers are alcoholics, in the sense that they are addicted to alcohol; (2) alcohol addicts will drink something like the biological maximum every day, practically regardless of the cost of obtaining their drinks; (3) therefore, it must be the more moderate drinkers who adapt their drinking practices to the price of alcoholic beverages.

This sort of argument may seem plausible to many. In reply, an economist would point out that a price increase has a greater economic impact on an alcoholic—who may already be spending a third or more of his or her income on alcohol—than on a moderate drinker, and that ordinarily this greater impact would be expected to yield, if anything, a greater response in consumption behavior. Furthermore, there is considerable clinical evidence that alcohol consumption by alcoholics is responsive to experimental manipulations of the costs of taking a drink (Mello, 1972; Nathan and Lisman, 1976). In any event, this issue can be better resolved through careful empirical analysis than through unsupported generalizations about the behavior in question.

The Effect of Alcohol Taxes on Cirrhosis Mortality   Statistics on the prevalence of chronic heavy drinking are not widely available. However, there is a widely accepted proxy measure—the rate of deaths due to cirrhosis of the liver. These death rates have provided the basis for nearly all estimates of alcoholism prevalence rates (Seeley, 1960).

Most people who die of liver cirrhosis, especially after age 30, exhibit a history of chronic intense drinking: Schmidt (1977) found that 80 percent of all cirrhosis deaths in Ontario in 1974 were alcohol-related. The typical victim of alcohol-related cirrhosis has consumed an enormous amount of alcohol; Lelbach (1974) estimates that a primarily healthy, 150-pound person who drinks roughly 21 ounces of 86 proof liquor every day for about 20 years has a 50 percent chance of contracting liver cirrhosis. Thus, for any one individual, there tends to be a long lag between the onset of heavy drinking and the prospect of death from liver cirrhosis. The cirrhosis mortality rate is therefore not a direct indicator of the current fraction of alcoholics in a population, but does give a good indication of the fraction that has been drinking heavily for two or more decades. It should be kept in mind that the cirrhosis mortality rate is of interest in its own right, in addition to being a proxy for the prevalence of alcoholism. Cirrhosis is among the leading causes of death in the United States, Canada, and most European nations.

Using this statistical indicator of the prevalence of chronic excess consumption, it is possible to explore the relationship between alcohol taxes and excess drinking. My first study of this relationship (Cook, 1981) was based on annual observations of 30 states for the 15-year period spanning 1960 to 1974. During this period there were 38 instances in which one of these states increased its liquor tax by a substantial amount (more than $.24 per proof gallon). I viewed each of these tax increases as a test case in a sort of "natural experiment." For each of these test cases, the percentage change in the state's cirrhosis mortality rate was calculated; the test statistic was defined as the mortality rate during the 3 years before the tax increase. The control groups for each of these test cases were the other states in the corresponding years. The result was that states that raised their liquor tax typically had a greater reduction (or smaller increase) in cirrhosis mortality than other states in the corresponding year (see Table 3-1). Indeed, 63 percent of all test cases were in the upper half of the distribution with respect to the test statistic—a result that would occur by chance alone with probability .072. This result is fairly strong evidence that the tax increase reduced the cirrhosis mortality rate, at least in the short run.

Why did some (38 percent) of the states with increased taxes experience a relative increase in cirrhosis mortality? My interpretation is that cirrhosis mortality fluctuates from year to year for a variety of reasons besides changes in liquor prices. In some of the test cases, these chance fluctuations happened to be positive and large enough to more than compensate for the consumption-suppressing effect of the tax increase. The fact that in most cases (63 percent) the state exhibited a relative reduction in cirrhosis mortality suggests that this effect does exist.

The principal challenge to the validity of this interpretation is that a state legislature's decision to raise the tax is influenced, directly or indirectly, by cirrhosis trends in the state. For example, if a sudden increase in cirrhosis mortality led to a tax increase and a natural regression to the cirrhosis mortality trend subsequently occurred, then the tax increase would be followed by a reduction in mortality but would not necessarily have caused it. This possibility is tested in Cook (1981) and Cook and Tauchen (1982). The evidence from these tests does not support this interpretation of my result—tax increases apparently *are* largely exogenous.

My quasi-experimental approach to studying the effect of liquor taxes on heavy drinkers has the virtues of simplicity and ease of interpreta-

TABLE 3-1   Effect of State Liquor Tax Increases on
Cirrhosis Mortality Rates, 1960-1974

Rank Order	Number of Test Cases	Percentage of Test Cases
1–5	9 ⎫	
6–10	9 ⎬	63.2
11–15	6 ⎭	
16–20	3 ⎫	
21–25	9 ⎬	36.8
26–30	2 ⎭	

Note: For each year during the sample period, the 30 states are
rank ordered with respect to percentage change in cirrhosis
mortality rate. The state with the largest reduction is ranked first.
States that raised their taxes were usually at the low end (with the
greatest reductions) of this distribution in the year of the tax
increase.

Source: Cook (1981:277).

tion. It does not generate a usable estimate of the magnitude of the
effect in question, however. Primarily for this reason I undertook a
second study (Cook and Tauchen, 1982), which applied an estimation
technique (analysis of covariance estimated by generalized least squares
regression) to annual data from the same 30 states for the period 1962-
1977. Before undertaking this task, we refined the annual state-level
cirrhosis mortality data; our variable was the age-adjusted mortality
rate for state residents ages 30 and over. Our principal result can be
stated this way: other things being equal, a $1 per proof gallon increase
in a state's liquor tax will reduce the state's cirrhosis mortality rate by
1.9 percent in the short run. (The tax variable in the regression was
adjusted for inflation, as measured by the consumer price index. The
statement of our results given here is converted to October 1981 dollars.)
The 95 percent confidence interval for this estimated reduction is 0.4-
3.5 percent; thus our parameter estimate is statistically significant by
the usual standards of social science. Our parameter estimate suggests
further that the tax effect is far from trivial—according to this estimate,
a doubling of the U.S. federal liquor tax would reduce the nation's
cirrhosis mortality rate by a figure in the neighborhood of 20 percent.

Given the normally long lag between the onset of heavy drinking and
death from cirrhosis, it may not be obvious how an increase in the liquor
tax could cause an immediate reduction in cirrhosis mortality. The
reason is that the cirrhotic process is interruptible—if at any time an
alcoholic should stop drinking, his or her liver would cease to deterio-

rate. If the rate of consumption slows, then the deterioration process also slows. At any one time, there is a reservoir of people who are within one year of death from cirrhosis at their current rate of consumption. If some of them reduce their consumption in response to a tax increase, then not all of them will die in that year—i.e., the mortality rate will decline in the first year. What about the trend in mortality over the long run? The mortality rate will gradually decline after the initial drop, as the size of the reservoir gradually shrinks. The total effect of the tax increase will not be realized for many years, but clearly the ultimate reduction in mortality rates due to such an increase will exceed the initial reduction. Thus, our figures underestimate the full effect.

In conclusion, there is considerable statistical evidence that a liquor tax increase causes an immediate and substantial reduction in cirrhosis mortality. If cirrhosis mortality rates are a reliable indicator of the prevalence of alcoholism, then it can be inferred that alcoholics' drinking habits are quite sensitive to the price of liquor.

The Effect of Liquor Taxes on Auto Fatalities   There is also some direct evidence that accident rates are responsive to changes in the liquor tax. I tested the effect of state liquor tax increases on the auto fatality rate in my 1981 paper, using the same sample and technique as those in the cirrhosis study. Between 1960 and 1974, most of the states (25 of 38) that increased their liquor tax subsequently experienced a below-average change in auto fatality rates relative to states that did not increase their tax.

Unfortunately there is no comparable evidence on the effect of beer prices on auto fatalities. Beer is particularly important because it is the beverage of choice for the demographic group posing the greatest risk on our highways—young people.

Conclusion   Available evidence suggests that increases in alcoholic beverage taxes cause reductions in per capita consumption, consumption by chronic heavy drinkers, and the incidence of drunken driving. It seems safe to conclude that the sharp decline in alcohol prices during the last 15 years has exacerbated alcohol-related public health problems. Fortunately there appear to have been countervailing forces at work during this period, such as increased emphasis in the popular culture on health and fitness, that have prevented a large increase in drinking from occurring. Indeed, adult per capita consumption has changed very little since 1970. If alcohol prices had kept pace with inflation, the per capita consumption would probably have declined substantially during this period.

Equity Considerations in Alcoholic Beverage Taxation

Alcohol control policies, including taxation, have been criticized by some as excessively blunt instruments, reducing the enjoyment of the many for the sake of curtailing the alcohol-related problems suffered by the relatively few. In the imagery of Gusfield (1976:275), these policies fall "like sober rain from heaven upon the problem and problem-free drinkers alike." There are two comments to be made in response to this critique.

First, much of the social cost of excess drinking also falls on "the problem and problem-free drinkers alike," as well as the abstainers. Our government social insurance tax rates and private auto and health insurance premiums reflect, in part, the costly consequences of alcohol abuse. The drunk driver puts all of us at increased risk of an injury or death on the highway. Thus, it can be argued that an effective alcohol control measure will indirectly benefit the problem-free drinkers (as well as those who abstain) by reducing the collective costs generated by problem drinking.

Second, the direct costs of alcohol control measures such as taxation are more or less proportional to the amount of alcohol an individual consumes—the "sober rain" falls on all drinkers, but with much greater intensity on the chronic heavy drinkers than on others. In the United States it is estimated that the heaviest-drinking 10 percent of the adult population consumes about 57 percent of all beverage alcohol sold each year (Gerstein, 1981:193). To the extent that alcohol taxes are proportional to ethanol content, then, this top group of drinkers will also pay 57 percent of the taxes. Thus, the relatively small group of drinkers who have the highest incidence of alcohol-related problems also pays the bulk of the alcohol taxes.

To summarize, alcohol taxes, if effective in reducing the costly consequences of excess consumption, reduce the burden alcohol imposes on society at large. Furthermore, whether or not alcohol taxes are effective in reducing the costly consequences of excess consumption, they have the characteristic of exacting payment in proportion to consumption and hence (very roughly) in proportion to the social costs generated by their consumption. If we believe that the drinker should pay (at least in an actuarial sense) for the social costs related to his or her drinking, then the excise tax on alcohol is reasonably efficient.

A second equity issue concerns the burden imposed on poor households by alcohol taxes. Such taxes are of course not adjusted to the household's ability to pay (as is the income tax), and by a traditional measure alcohol taxes appear regressive. However, it is certainly possible that an increase in alcohol taxes will actually prove beneficial to the children of the heavy drinkers in poor families. For example, if a household's demand for alcoholic beverages is elastic (price elasticity greater than 1.0), an increase in price will cause a reduction in total expenditures on drinking, thereby leaving more money for other household expenditures. Surely poor households vary considerably with respect to price elasticity of demand. However, the available evidence suggests that the average household's demand for liquor is quite elastic; furthermore, poor households would tend to be more elastic than higher-income households. Therefore, for some fraction of poor households, an increase in alcohol tax rates would reduce expenditures on alcoholic beverages. And, it is quite possible that a tax-induced reduction in

TABLE 3-2   Revenue Effects of Changing Federal Alcohol Excise Taxes: Proportional Increases

	Current		"Doubling" Option		"Restore to 1951 Levels" Option[a]	
	Excise Tax Rate	Tax Collections[b] (billions)	Tax Collections Zero Elasticity (billions)	Tax Collections Unit Elasticity (billions)	Tax Collections Zero Elasticity (billions)	Tax Collections Unit Elasticity (billions)[c]
Liquor (86 proof fifth)	1.81	3.94	7.89	6.35	14.86	8.90
Beer (six-pack)[d]	.16	1.49	2.98	2.82	5.61	4.84
Wine (gallon, 12% alcohol)[e]	.17	.21	.41	.41	.78	.76
Increase in revenues		0	5.64	3.94	15.62	8.86

[a]The price level in March 1983 exceeded the 1951 price level by a factor of 3.77.
[b]From 1979.
[c]These calculations assume that the own price elasticity of demand is unity for all three beverage types, with zero cross-price elasticities. Assumed prices were $7.50 per fifth for liquor, $2.80 per six-pack, and $8 per gallon of wine.
[d]The federal excise tax on beer is $9 per 31-gallon barrel, implying a $0.16 tax per 72-oz. six-pack.
[e]Wine tax rates are higher for fortified and sparkling wines.

consumption by heavy-drinking household heads may benefit other family members insofar as reduced drinking yields improved health and higher earnings.

Federal Revenues and Tax Rates

Currently federal excise tax collections on alcoholic beverages are about $6 billion. Table 3-2 provides estimates of the revenue effects from increasing excise tax rates uniformly on all three beverage tax rates. For example, if Congress were to double alcohol excise taxes (as they did cigarette taxes in 1982), a reasonable estimate of the revenue increase is $4 billion in the first year. The assumption behind this estimate is that the demand function for each beverage type is characterized by a constant elasticity of 1. (Revenue estimates for beer and wine are not sensitive to changes in this assumption.) Under the same assumption, revenue would increase by about $9 billion if Congress were to return alcohol beverage tax rates to 1951 levels in real terms.

Instead of increasing all three excise tax rates proportionately, Congress might be well advised to standardize tax rates per ounce of ethanol across all beverage types. Under the current tax structure, liquor is taxed at $.164 per ounce of ethanol, whereas the tax on beer is equivalent to about $.057 per ounce, and table wine about $.011 per ounce. Raising beer and wine taxes to the level of the liquor tax would bring in more revenue than doubling all tax rates and would have the important advantage of giving official recognition to the principle that ethanol is the problem agent, regardless of the type of beverage in which it is contained.

Conclusion

The decline in the real value of the U.S. federal excise taxes on alcoholic beverages has benefited heavy drinkers in some ways but has had the effect of increasing the prevalence of alcoholism and its attendant costs. Raising the excise tax would be a rather well-targeted response to the social burden that heavy drinkers as a group impose on the rest of society. There are a number of alternatives for reducing the U.S. budget deficit. Few of them have the substantial beneficial side effects that would result from raising the alcohol excise tax rates.

MORE DATA ON TAX POLICY

JEFFREY E. HARRIS, Massachusetts Institute of Technology

My comments are fivefold. First, I show that the tax burden on alcohol has been declining at all levels of government. Second, I attempt to shed some additional light on the possible relation between alcohol excise tax rates and cirrhosis mortality rates. Third, I demonstrate that alcoholic beverage taxation is not a highly regressive policy, as is sometimes claimed. Fourth, I explain why the current design of differential taxes on beer, wine, and liquor is a complex problem. Finally, I suggest that ad valorem taxation of alcoholic beverages is a practical alternative to current excise tax policy.

Local, State, and Federal Tax Burdens on Alcoholic Beverages

The tax burden on alcoholic beverages has declined considerably in the past two decades. From 1965 to 1980, as shown in Table 3-3, federal alcohol tax revenues declined from 3.6 to 1.4 percent of total federal tax receipts, while state and local government alcohol tax revenues declined from 1.8 to 1.2 percent of total receipts. Tax payments from alcoholic beverages also constituted a declining proportion of excise tax revenues. As shown in Table 3-1, combined tax revenues from alcohol for all levels of government fell from 14.0 percent of excise tax receipts in 1965 to 6.3 percent in 1980.

When corrected for inflation, annual alcohol tax payments per adult fell by 50 percent during 1965-1980.

Cirrhosis Mortality and Taxes: Cook's Argument Reconsidered

Cook and Tauchen (1982) have estimated that an increase in the liquor excise tax of $1 (in current dollars) per proof gallon would reduce the mortality rate from cirrhosis of the liver by 1.9 percent in the short run and perhaps by twice that amount in the long run. With the current federal excise tax on liquor at $10.50 proof per gallon, a doubling of the federal tax rate would reduce the cirrhosis mortality by a predicted 20 percent.

The effect measured by Cook and Tauchen was not estimated too precisely. Thus, the predicted 20 percent short-run decline in cirrhosis mortality has an overall 95 percent confidence range of about 5-40 percent. Still, the effect estimated by Cook and Tauchen is extraordinarily large. A 20 percent decline in the U.S. cirrhosis mortality would be about twice the proportional decline in mortality experienced during 1968-1978. (The age-adjusted death rates for cirrhosis of the liver were

TABLE 3-3   Tax Burden on Alcoholic Beverages in the United
States

Category	Year			
	1965- 1966	1970- 1971	1975- 1976	1980- 1981
Alcohol tax revenues ($ billions)				
Federal	3.7	4.8	5.4	5.7
State and local	1.0	1.6	2.2	2.8
All government	4.7	6.4	7.6	8.5
Alcohol tax revenues as percentage of total tax receipts (percent)				
Federal	3.6	3.5	2.7	1.4
State and local	1.8	1.7	1.4	1.2
All government	2.9	2.7	2.1	1.3
Alcohol tax revenues as percentage of sales and excise tax receipts (percent)				
Federal	25.3	24.6	24.9	11.7
State and local	5.3	4.8	4.0	3.3
All government	14.0	12.1	9.9	6.3
Per capita alcohol tax payments ($)	36	45	49	50
Per capita alcohol tax payments in constant dollars (1967)	38	38	29	19

Notes: Sales and excise taxes include general sales and gross receipts taxes; custom
duties; motor fuel taxes; alcoholic beverage, tobacco products, and public utilities
taxes; and other excise taxes including (in 1980-1981 only) the windfall profits tax. Per
capita quantities based on noninstitutional population ages 16 years and over.
Adjustment to constant dollars used the consumer price index for all items.

Source: U.S. Bureau of Commerce, Government finances, selected years. *Economic
Report of the President 1983,* Appendix B. Washington, D.C.: U.S. Department of
Commerce.

13.9 per 100,000 in 1968 and 12.4 per 100,000 in 1978.) Thus, a 20 percent decline would mean a postponement of about 6,000 deaths annually.

Is an effect of this magnitude conceivable? A doubling of the federal tax rate, if fully passed on to consumers, would constitute an approximate 24 percent increase in the retail price of liquor. (For example, the increased tax would raise the retail price of a fifth of 86 proof liquor from about $7.50 to about $9.30.) Hence, according to Cook and Tauchen, each 1 percent increase in the current retail price of liquor is estimated to reduce cirrhosis mortality by about 0.8 percent in the short run alone. Social scientists have estimated that a 1 percent increase in price reduces overall alcohol consumption by about 1 percent (see the studies cited in Cook and Tauchen, 1982). If the cirrhosis mortality rate is a reasonable index of the extent of heavy drinking, then the estimates imply that heavy drinkers are about as price-sensitive as the general population. Since more than half the alcohol in the United States is bought by about one-tenth of the population (Moore and Gerstein, 1981), this may not be unreasonable.

A decline in the mortality rate from cirrhosis of the liver could reflect either a decline in the prevalence of cirrhosis or a reduction in the death rate among established cirrhotics. Powell and Klatskin (1968) found the 5-year survival of cirrhotics to be 40.5 percent among those who continued to drink and 63.0 percent among those who stopped using alcohol. The differential survival in the first year after alcohol cessation, however, was only about 1 percent. The estimated difference in survival is necessarily sensitive to the stage of the disease at the time of cessation of alcohol. (Powell and Klatskin included only liver biopsy-proven cirrhotics who came to their attention as a result of certain clinical signs.) Still, the data suggest that an effect of the magnitude estimated by Cook and Tauchen would be mainly the influence of price on the prevalence of cirrhosis.

Several additional lines of research are needed to fill in the gaps in the taxation-cirrhosis story. First, it would be desirable to study the effects of price at the individual level, as has been done for cigarette use (Harris, 1980, 1982; Lewit and Coate, 1982). In the case of cigarettes, increased taxes affect smoking participation rates more than they affect the number of cigarettes smoked by continuing smokers. In particular, a high cigarette price may also dissuade young people from starting to smoke (Lewit et al., 1981). Whether an alcohol price increase might affect behavior in these or other ways is worthy of serious study.

Second, the cross-responsiveness of demand for various types of beverages needs to be studied. If an increase in the liquor tax alone would result in a substantial shift in demand to beer and wine, then the

TABLE 3-4 Alcohol Use According to Family Income, Persons Ages 17 and Older

Annual Family Income	Alcohol Use (Percentage)			
	Never Use	Light Use	Moderate Use	Heavy Use
Less than $5,000	43	42	12	3
$5,000-$9,999	32	49	16	3
$10,000-$14,999	24	53	19	4
$15,000-$24,999	19	54	23	4
$25,000 or more	13	55	27	5
All incomes (incl. unknown)	25	52	19	4

Notes: Never Use: Denies current use of wine, beer, or liquor.
   Light Use: Up to 0.5 drinks per day.
   Moderate Use: Up to 2.0 drinks per day.
   Heavy Use: Exceeding 2.0 drinks per day.
Total drinks computed from the number of drinking days per week and the number of drinks per sitting. Drinks of beer, wine, and liquor weighted equally.

Source: U.S. National Center for Health Statistics, unpublished data from 22,842 respondents, Health Interview Survey, 1977.

effect measured by Cook and Tauchen (which, I assume, depends only on liquor tax increases) would be even more remarkable.

Third, we need to know what is happening to the prevalence of non-alcohol-related cirrhosis in the United States, particularly those forms of the disease caused by non-A, non-B hepatitis virus and by certain hepatotoxic drugs. We also need to know more about recent trends in the survival of cirrhotics, particularly with the increased availability and quality of medical care since 1965. Does the cirrhosis death rate still accurately track the extent of heavy alcohol use?

Finally, the relations between taxes and other alcohol-related endpoints need to be studied further. Alcohol-related traffic casualties and hospital discharges, admissions to alcohol rehabilitation facilities, and deaths from alcohol overdose come to mind.

Tax Equity Revisited

Table 3-4 shows the relation between alcohol use and family income among adults responding to the 1977 Health Interview Survey, conducted by the U.S. National Center for Health Statistics. My method of measuring the extent of alcohol use from these data may differ from those used in other surveys. Moreover, respondents to such surveys probably understate the extent of their alcohol use (though it is unclear whether the degree of underreporting is related to income). Still, the evidence shows that alcohol is a luxury good, that is, one for which consumption markedly increases with income. As in the case of tobacco (Harris, 1982; Harris, unpublished data), the reduced consumption at very low incomes reflects to some degree a large number of older, low-income abstainers. Even when age is taken into account, however, alcohol use increases with income.

In view of the cited data it is hard to make the case that alcohol taxation is highly regressive. As in the case of cigarette taxation, an increase in alcohol taxes would be a means of raising revenues with minimal burden on the elderly.

With respect to the economic burden of taxation on the family of an alcoholic or heavy drinker, Cook has noted that when a consumer's use of alcohol is sufficiently sensitive to price, an increase in price actually causes a net decrease in his total expenditure on alcohol. Therefore, among very heavy drinkers, if higher prices dissuade a sufficient quantity of drinking, then there is a net saving in the family budget.

Taxing Beer, Wine, and Liquor Differentially

The tax per unit alcohol varies widely across beverage types (Moore and Gerstein, 1981). Per unit weight of alcohol, the federal excise tax on wine is about one-fifteenth that of liquor, and the federal tax on beer is about one-third. At current prices, equalization of the tax per unit alcohol would require about a $0.30 increase in the price of a six-pack of beer and about a $2.40 increase in the price of a gallon of wine.

If the damage from alcoholic beverage use depends solely on the quantity consumed, then shouldn't the tax rates per unit alcohol be equalized across beverage types? The answer is complicated. Let me give three examples: Suppose that alcohol enhanced the risk of traffic accidents most notably among those who preferred their alcohol in the form of beer. Then, other things being equal, the tax per unit alcohol on beer should be higher. Similarly, if alcohol is most damaging to health among heavy users, who preferred liquor, then the tax per unit alcohol on liquor should be higher. Finally, suppose that the purported salutary effects of alcohol use on the risks of coronary heart disease accrue mainly to light drinkers of wine. Then the tax per unit alcohol on wine should be lower.

The issue here is not whether the harm from alcoholic beverages depends, for any one person, solely on the quantity of alcohol. Instead, we need to know the correlation across consumers between alcohol-related damages and alcoholic beverage preferences (Harris, 1980).

The Ad Valorem Alternative

The prospect of large future budget deficits even if the current economic recovery should accelerate has heightened interest in the use of excise and sales taxes to raise new revenues. In such an economic environment those favoring the use of increased alcohol taxes to reduce alcohol-related damage should propose some form of ad valorem taxation. A tax levied as a fixed proportion of the wholesale price of alcoholic beverages would avoid the need for periodic new tax increases to keep pace with inflation.

COMMENTS ON TAX POLICY

MARY HEVENER, U.S. Department of the Treasury

Dr. Cook made a very good point: much of the legislative interest in the area of alcohol excise taxes originates because they are a source of revenue. The federal liquor excise tax raises $4 billion, which is not an insignificant amount of money. But in the 2 years I have been in the U.S. Treasury's tax policy office, there has been very little legislation to review in this area. The only substantive legislation that has been subject to hearings on Capitol Hill has been a bill to repeal the existing excise tax on liquor "stills," which we supported because it cost $90,000 to administer the tax and only raised about $70,000.

Still, in working on various alcohol excise tax proposals, I have been a little troubled that the major consideration in reviewing the proposals is simply dollars. One proposal that surfaced briefly in 1982 was to increase by a tiny amount the existing excise taxes on liquor in order to fund a nationwide anti–drunk-driving program. I received a call from the Hill with questions about the current level of alcohol consumption and what the effect of a truly minuscule increase in alcohol excise taxes—pennies a gallon—would be in an effort to raise $30 or $40 million to fund the anti–drunk-driving program. It was an interesting proposal because it was not geared simply to raising revenue, but to funding a social program. It was very difficult to find any information on three hours' notice; as a tax attorney, my sources are largely the Internal Revenue Code and regulations thereunder, which do not yield much information about alcohol consumption or the effects of excise tax increases on cirrhosis of the liver.

When congressional consideration was given in 1982 to increasing excise taxes in an effort to raise revenues, I understand that Congress briefly considered increasing alcohol instead of tobacco excise taxes (which were ultimately increased). Consideration was given to exempting beer from any increase: in the opinion of the staff—formulated statistically by inquiring what people in the room thought would be the impact—the beer tax was deemed more regressive than the others, beer being "the elixir of the working man." Not much research was done by the tax lawyers who were putting together the statute; in the press of legislation, there is not time to hold hearings and elicit studies.

In my opinion—not to be taken as an official position of the administration nor of the U.S. Treasury—the focus in presenting recommendations for legislative change should be wider than simply balancing the budget; it should reflect the health and social concerns voiced here. The materials from this conference could be quite useful in preparing future revenue estimates and testimony, which, as a result, might reflect the estimated social and medical effects of any proposed alcohol excise tax change.

THOMAS TURNER, Johns Hopkins Alcohol Research Center

We have been hearing about tax matters here from two standpoints: revenue and health. I assume that it is not our business, as a group, to solve this country's fiscal problems. We should concentrate on health effects. It is an attractive but not proven idea that health benefits can flow from an increase in taxation. Relatively few taxes have been directly imposed for health reasons. I believe in other countries—especially Norway and Australia—it has occurred that as taxes increased, alcohol production became a cottage industry, so what is measured there might not be total consumption at all. For a decade there has been an epidemic of viral hepatitis as well as a fair amount of drug-induced liver damage in this country. These cases are now declining. There is evidence that moderate drinking has some beneficial effects. We therefore have to be careful in measuring presumed alcohol effects, including the cirrhosis rate, in this country. I'm not certain that taxes are going to deter such effects, and the report is careful not to say "this is a proven fact."

CHARLES CRAWFORD, Gallo Winery

The baseline on the statement that excise taxes have not been raised was 1951. But we had no tax at all on wine during Prohibition. Between 1940 and 1951 the federal tax on table wine increased 240 percent, on dessert wine 570 percent, and on sparkling wine 750 percent. If one took 1940 as the baseline, excise taxes would appear to have kept up with other costs.

I have gone over the work presented by Dr. Cook, and I believe his conclusions require more data and a longer lag time. Dr. Cook indicates that his is a "quasi-experimental approach"; I think it should not be used to make decisions on tax changes. I think we need to put far more emphasis on individual initiative and social responsibility.

JOHN VASSALLO, JR., State of New Jersey

It is my belief that consumption can be cut down among those who are not abusive users of alcohol, but that taxes and prices, no matter how they are raised, will not affect the drinking habits of alcoholics. Increased prices and taxes will only cause alcoholics—and for that matter social drinkers, occasional users, or persons who purchase for use at parties but not for themselves—to purchase less expensive brands. It may have some effect on the consumption of those who are relatively indifferent toward alcoholic beverages, but I do not believe it will have an appreciable effect on alcoholics. At the same time, the decrease in consumption that does occur will affect the overall tax picture. Raising taxes may not in fact create additional revenue for a state. It could even create a negative tax impact, and alcoholic beverage taxes or profits (in the control states) are very important to the economy of almost every state.

ROGER THOMSON, S & A Restaurant Corporation

There must be some sort of balancing. The restaurant and tavern business employs many people. The income taxes that these employees pay are substantial. Most states and the federal government, to which my own firm paid several million dollars last year, are more than happy to tax our receipts. The revenue that excise taxes raise may have some side effects, such as decreasing sales, loss of some employees, and corresponding loss of revenue. There may not be as many restaurants built, and those property taxes will be lost. It is just not quite as simple as raising the taxes to gain extra money.

DAVID KRAFT, University of Massachusetts, Amherst

I have reluctantly been persuaded that an increase in excise taxes is a reasonable approach and will cut down on alcohol problems. My question is: How long is the effect? There may be an initial immediate effect with a tailing off, depending on how the tax legislation is written.

DAN BEAUCHAMP, University of North Carolina

That is true if it is a flat excise tax, not ad valorem. I think part of our charter as individual citizens is to think about whether this approach is feasible. I am impressed with how difficult it is to get a state legislature to raise alcohol taxes unless there is some kind of emergency. Various reasons are given to not raise taxes: people might cross the border to other states; legislators are concerned that the poor should not be penalized. But as long as alcohol is available, as I believe it should be, we are never going to be without alcohol problems in this society. Since we cannot eliminate alcohol problems, we should think about making them somewhat smaller.

I think an excise tax increase is attractive, and it could be the most important measure in the preventive realm. It appeals to me because it is a measure for which we have some clear evidence, in an uncertain world, that two good things would happen: revenues would increase, and there would be important health benefits. This evidence is convincing for the improvement in cirrhosis, more tentative in the case of fatal highway crashes.

Taxation has the clear advantage of working at a distance from people and accomplishing more than one end, which in politics is always good. Taxation has one other effect that we should all hold in mind: A full slate of programs that are purely educational in focus will no doubt do some good, but if a six-pack of beer in a supermarket costs roughly the same as a six-pack of Coca-Cola, all the educational programs you can design fly in the face of that fact. Soft drinks and beer now sell at roughly the same price; this was not true 15 years ago. The cost of nonalcoholic beverages has more than tripled in the same period that the cost of alcoholic beverages has less than doubled, and we now see price convergence of the two. This has much to do with government policy on sugar and alcohol. We have seen great increases in the cost of essential goods, partly as a result of government policy, while alcohol stays cheap. Is this sound public policy? I think not.

In spite of the earlier history that Mr. Crawford alluded to, the tax level in the days of Eisenhower was roughly three times what it is now. If I changed nothing else, I would change that.

Prevention is a zero-sum game, in the sense that the alcohol beverage industry will have to lose something if these measures work. I can understand perfectly why the industry does not want that, but there is not much more to say than that it looks like it works. We should just confess the fact that it is going to hurt a very important, influential industry—not as much as they fear, I think, but it is going to hurt.

FRANK KENEL, American Automobile Association

We have done that with the automotive industry. Like it or not, auto safety has cost jobs. I have no quarrel with it; I favor what has happened in terms of the life-saving benefits. I think other industries will have to do the same thing.

LAWRENCE WALLACK, University of California, Berkeley

Tax policy is one piece of an overall prevention strategy that would deemphasize the use of alcohol in our society. The direction of current excise and other tax provisions actually encourages greater use of alcohol. An effective tax policy would say, "Alcohol has a special status in society because it is a drug, and the Surgeon General says it contributes to (not necessarily causes) as many as one out of ten deaths." An effective policy would condition the environment to make it more supportive of those who want to drink moderately, more supportive of people who do not want to drink at all, and more supportive of parents' interests. One part of our policy dealing with alcohol should support the other parts of our policy. For example, it does not make sense to have enormous amounts of misinformation in much of the advertising we see, and then to have people working on a voluntary basis to convince kids that the multi-million-dollar effort telling them that drinking is good is not quite right. I think we have to look at it from many different vantage points. Tax policy is not the single answer. Anyone who thinks that there is a single answer has missed the whole point of the National Research Council report.

TAX POLICY AND LEGISLATIVE COALITIONS

MICHAEL FOX, Ohio General Assembly

As a politician and a legislator who for nine years has been trying to sort out data from groups like the National Research Council and translate them into public policy, it is refreshing to start with some very specific information about the consequences of actual policy options. I think the next question to be addressed as we look at tax policy, whether at the state or federal level, is: What is the context in which the battle will occur?

The Context of Policy Formation

The context in Washington, D.C., is a little different from the context in Ohio or Connecticut or any of the states. The policy goals are different. There is a difference between control (or monopoly) and noncontrol states. I am from one of the control or monopoly states, where we control the wholesale and retail distribution of spiritous liquors. That changes somewhat the building of coalitions in the legislative process for any policy affecting alcohol. Within the state there are certain subgroups with different objectives, which sometimes make for strange bedfellows in the pursuit of rational public policy. So I speak from my own bias and experience in a control state in discussing from a practical standpoint some of the options and some of the problems in translating research data into public policy.

As I reflect on the comments of Dr. Cook and others regarding the use of tax policy to affect consumption, I have to note that two months ago I discussed the very same question with a lobbyist representing Miller Brewery. The lobbyist argued against a certain tax proposal in Ohio, saying that it would affect Miller adversely; since he was talking to a legislator who represents a county in which Miller Brewery had just built about $500 million worth of brewing facility, he was a little distraught that I would suggest taxing his product.

The brewers had conducted a survey of beer consumption and public policy in 17 states. Their study found the most pronounced effect of policy on consumption in Michigan. Two events occurred simultaneously there that resulted in roughly a 6 percent drop in consumption: a 10-cent deposit tax and an increase in the drinking age to 21. Indiana recently increased its excise tax on beer and wine and found that in the 2-3 month period immediately following the increase in the excise tax, there was a demonstrable drop in consumption. But after that period, observed consumption started matching over time what their normal projections would have been.

If the main, publicly stated objective from a policy standpoint is to reduce consumption through taxation, I believe it will create substantial problems in building coalitions in the legislature. A lot of folks make a good living selling alcoholic beverages, and they have for years contended that tax policy affects consumption. I spent four years on the state government committee in Ohio, and all we heard in that committee were what we affectionately called "booze bills." One after another, the tavern owners and the wholesalers would come before us and say, "You are putting us out of business, this is affecting our sales." The traditional position of the advocacy groups in our state during this period was, "No, it will not affect your business, you will still be in business, but it will affect our ability to direct resources into programs for prevention and intervention." I mention this as a word of caution. There is a real world out there in which legislators get beat over the head. If a bill goes to a state government committee or a similar committee in one of the legislatures, it will have a hard time getting out of committee because such committees are dominated by people who are generally friendly to the industry.

A second problem is the public's perception. It has been mentioned that beer is considered the poor man's drink. When tax proposals are presented in the legislature, those who sell the product quickly team up with those who consume the product to champion the poor working person. Strange coalitions develop; when the United Auto Workers, the AFL-CIO, and other unions interested in policy development team up with industry, they seldom lack funds for getting their message communicated. The ability to influence public perception is an important consideration in translating research findings into public policy.

A Coalition-Building Proposal

I am involved in a proposal in Ohio to get the state out of the retail liquor business, give up its retail monopoly, and go to a "license" or "package store" concept for distribution. The legislative committee of the regional councils on alcoholism in Ohio now endorses this proposal, which they had traditionally opposed. The enticement was to put a 2-cent-a-drink tax increase before the legislature and earmark portions of that tax for treatment and prevention programs. Forty percent of that 2-cent-a-drink revenue stays local as a block grant to deal with the results of abuse of the product, a plan that brought support from the municipal league and county commissioner groups. These are the people struggling to deal with legislation we passed a year ago saying, "We want drunk drivers off the road and in jail." The local governments did not have the resources to carry out that legislation, and right now it is like a meat market—"Take a number and in a year or so we will tell you if there is a jail cell for you." We put another 10 percent of the revenue directly into alcohol abuse programs, another 10 percent into school and education-based prevention, another 10 percent exclusively into drug prevention, and 30 percent into the state's general revenue fund.

I see this proposal first as a budget and fiscal issue. The cost of running the retail distribution portion of the Department of Liquor Control is currently $35 million a year; inventory management is another $30 million a year. The net effect of getting the state out of the liquor business and imposing the 2-cent-a-drink tax—not counting the dedicated revenue or the revenue that would stay local or the revenue that we would earmark to alcohol prevention and intervention programs and drug prevention and intervention programs in the schools—would mean a net revenue increase for the state over a 2-year period of $221 million.

We knew that tavern owners and retailers would oppose the 2-cent-a-drink tax. They have an armlock on the state government committee, and no proposal could get through that committee unless it mobilized equal firepower. So we went to the grocery chains and said, "If you want to sell this stuff, what we have to offer is the combination of a 2-cent-a-drink tax and getting the state out of the retail business." They were very cautious. They did not want the negative public relations that might arise from being out front on the issue unless they knew where Mothers Against Drunk Drivers (MADD) was going to stand. The president of the state MADD organization has endorsed the proposal and the other councils on alcoholism have followed suit, so we may now have the firepower to get it through. We have formed a coalition of the retail merchants with an interest in selling the product and the activist and civic official groups that are attracted to the shared revenue arrangement. Without that firepower I do not think we could dream of getting this proposal through the legislature. We have at least 40 lobbyists in Ohio who meet with legislators to tell them we ought to leave this product alone. Our coalition has reduced the opposition basically to the tavern owners, and I would fight that battle politically any time. The odds are still against the proposal, but close enough to be worth fighting for.

In conclusion, policy objectives and public polls have to be translated into coalitions, which can be built on diverse bases. Revenue is one common concern. Another is the rising cost of health care. A third is criminal legislation: chiefs of police, local sheriffs, fraternal orders of police, judges, and so forth are very interested in penal legislation. There is tremendous coalition-building potential over the concern about young people's involvement with alcohol. The opportunity to greatly expand government partnerships with the private sector, with respect to alcohol and substance abuse, has never been better. The visibility given this issue by groups like MADD and by campaigns to make the public aware of the social costs and consequences of the abuse of this product have created an opportunity to move and move quickly.

If you can design a coordinated strategy to incorporate all these factors, you will have built the base, the numbers, the power to confront opposing forces in the legislature. Now is the time to gather banners that have not traditionally been used together as effectively as they could be. I do not know how long the opportunity for building coalitions will last, but I suggest that this opening be used to the fullest extent to create prevention-oriented public policy.

MORE COMMENTS ON THE POLICY PROCESS

DAN BEAUCHAMP, University of North Carolina

As I understand it, Mr. Fox, Ohio might become the first control state since Prohibition to deregulate. I hope that does not happen. Putting together a coalition of people who mainly represent the need for money in these dire times—prevention interests and segments of the industry who have an interest in deregulation—may be smart politics in the short run, but in my opinion, it would be detrimental to the public in the long run.

The first reason is revenue generation. James Mosher and I have done a study indicating that, generally, control states make much more money than they think they do from the monopoly system. They not only recoup the costs of running the warehouses and the distribution system, but also retain all the dollars that would go into profits and other things if the enterprise were totally private. In other words, they get more than just the tax; they also get the profits and other returns to private purveyors.

Second, while we do not have absolutely overwhelming evidence that the control states do a better all-around job of protecting the public than the license states, I think we will find, if we develop more precise instruments, that control states do a better job of controlling underage drinking. Underage purchases and falsified IDs are almost never found in the monopoly stores in my home state, North Carolina. I realize that is partly because monopoly stores do not carry beer. But I think that if you are concerned about teenage drinking, you do not want to lose the advantage you have in the control state on underage purchases.

As far as I can tell, if the deal in Ohio goes through, you may have a one-time political coalition that makes sense. But in the long run you are going to lose more control of the problem. I do not know whether in the details of the bill you are going to retain your fine system in Ohio of permitting only so many outlets per capita; if you are victorious, that system is still a good idea—I hope you do not throw it out. That is one of the more sensible policies we have in the United States.

So my comment is: I hope you lose. I understand your motivations politically in the short run, but in the long run the one interested group that is not at the table is the public. I have given testimony on taxing alcohol at legislative committees in North Carolina and generally I have observed three kinds of people there. First, there are many, many people from the industry. Second, there is the alcoholism constituency, which seeks money. Third, there are researchers interested in the effects of the total system on the health and safety of the public. The public itself is simply not paying attention to this issue, and you cannot mobilize them. I'm afraid a deregulatory environment is going to destroy 20 good systems in this country for controlling alcohol by making short-term deals that are politically smart but in the long term are going to be bad for the public.

MICHAEL FOX, Ohio General Assembly

I understand your goal and I think that if you read the legislation you would find that we agree rather than disagree. I cannot go into all the details, but let me note some of them.

First, on the revenue side, we will technically keep Ohio in the wholesale business. We will do that for reasons not related to alcohol policy, but to our liquor profits bonding program for economic development. We will retain—and the legislation requires that we generate in addition to the tax revenues—an amount of profit equal to the last fiscal year prior to the transition. Last year, that was a little over $103 million. We will retain that profit factor. The impact, in terms of the goal we are talking about here, will be a price increase, on the shelf, of about 20 percent. For the consuming public, who may think that package stores mean lower prices, that will not be the result in Ohio. That is the net effect when we add a 2-cent-an-ounce tax on liquor and maintain the policy that we retain wholesale profits equal to retail profits.

Second, no study indicates that the mode of distribution affects consumption—at least none that I have seen; if you have one, I want to see it. With regard to sales to minors in state-controlled stores, I do not know how things are arranged in North Carolina, but in Ohio the reason we do not have instances of violation in state-controlled stores is that in the last decade the Bureau of Liquor Control and the agents investigating false sales or sales to minors have been in the same department and have a private arrangement whereby they just do not "set up" state stores by sending in underage purchasers, which is the standard practice to get evidence solid enough to make a bust. There has not been one arrest in 10 years in our state system.

Finally, with respect to that sector of the public you think is not listening, I suggest that with the attention this issue has gotten nationally the public is now waiting to be mobilized, and MADD and other advocacy groups have already demonstrated their ability to do this. To achieve the goals we are talking about here, as a realistic matter, one has to be ready to compromise. To go into those committees and not have that coalition built, no matter how worthy the cause, is to lose.

The issue of increasing tax revenues is essential at this point for one key reason. Policies adopted by state legislatures across the country to get drunk drivers off the road will have sustained effects only to the degree that funds start to flow to the local communities to make sure that the policies can be carried out. We are seeing the short-run impact now in Ohio, where we recently enacted mandatory jail terms for drunk drivers. There is a fear that drunk drivers are going to be caught, and a lot of publicity about the courts breaking down under the load. But it is starting to seep through that we have a waiting list for jail cells. The pendulum will swing back to the other side, to water these efforts down and go back essentially to business as usual unless resources can be raised.

ALFRED MCALISTER, University of Texas Health Sciences Center

I want to illustrate that point further. In Texas, because of decreasing oil revenues, we have a mad scramble to find new revenues for the first time in many years. Our governor has seized on what we in Texas call sin taxes, referring of course to alcohol and tobacco taxes. It has become very clear that the political acceptability of such a tax increase depends on whether the public perceives some connection, an earmarking or diversion of a portion of the funds, to prevention programs. It is in a sense similar to the way that the administration in Washington rationalized the increased gasoline tax as a user fee. We are finding good evidence that not only the treatment interests, for example, that seek this money, but also the average taxpayer sees some political acceptability in it. Are there survey data to that effect?

GEORGE HACKER, Center for Science in the Public Interest

A number of surveys show that, without any prior education, a clear majority of the public favors increased, earmarked revenues from taxation of alcoholic beverages. Several surveys—one in South Carolina, one done by Gallup for the National Council on Alcoholism in New York, and the Harris polls—show that there is now growing public awareness, and non–alcohol-related organizations are developing an interest in alcohol tax and advertising issues.

For example, we at the Center for Science in the Public Interest are now coordinating the National Alcohol Tax Coalition, which involves the National Council on Alcoholism, drunk-driving prevention groups, and dozens of children's, elderly, family, consumer, health, church, and other non–alcohol-related groups. We have begun to act at the federal level to take advantage of deficit-reduction opportunities and the heightened public awareness about drunk driving. I think it is important that we not sit too long without recognizing that there are opportunities to mesh these diverse interests around a common interest.

ALFRED MCALISTER, University of Texas Health Sciences Center

Of course, the fate of these issues often boils down to what the head of the PTA and legislative lobbyists for health or medical associations and other pressure groups think, as opposed to what the voters think. People have a naive perception that the more the government earns on drinking, the less interest it may have in controlling the problem. There is a problem of voter education, of educating people and influencing their attitudes on these issues. One possible way of broadening the discussion would be to agree that if taxes are raised there is some logic to earmarking or diverting a portion of them to prevention. We could use a portion of any tax increase for a nationwide anti–drunk-driving campaign, for example. If a tax increase is not packaged right, the industry will try to make the drinker feel that it is onerous to him or her. In Texas we had a smoking campaign; the newspapers reported, "Health Group Wants Money from Smokers." It was being presented in the form of someone robbing someone else.

JANE SMITH PATTERSON, State of North Carolina

I am very concerned with legislators' perceptions of the alcohol issue. When dealing with a legislature, it is important to get across in a short amount of time, to people who come from very different backgrounds, the information necessary to make public policy. The task is something like talking to the child who returned from a prayer meeting and told her mother not to worry, the minister had said her quilt was on the way. The mother was puzzled, but the child insisted that that is what the minister had said. The next day, her mother learned that the text of the minister's lesson was, "Fear not, for thy Comforter is coming." Perception is critical.

One of the critical things is directing alcohol taxes into prevention efforts. In our state, we require at least 25 percent of the funds used on the alcohol effort in the total budget to go directly into prevention efforts. We would like to direct more into prevention efforts. This emphasis on prevention must come directly from the funding source.

Substantial responsibilities are now shifting to the states; therefore, substantial numbers of lobbyists are shifting to the states. In our current legislative session, more than 20 lobbyists are paid by liquor, beer, and wine interests. That is a considerable number to spend time persuading legislators of their particular points of view.

I think this is especially relevant to the proposition for equal taxation of alcohol products based on the amount of ethanol. This is appealing in that it recognizes that ethanol itself is the problem with these beverages, and therefore appears more equitable than the way we address the issue at present. But there is an even more important point for anyone working with a legislature: whatever the reasons for proposing this legislation—revenue, prevention efforts, or both—it splits the various lobbying interests from each other. Divide and conquer is something to use in trying to get any bill through a legislature.

To talk about dedicating federal excise taxes to the states to be spent on prevention is one thing. But at the state level, legislatures and governors across the country flatly dislike the earmarking of state revenues and will fight you even though they agree with what you want to do. They do not want funds to be dedicated in the actual excise tax act. They want the funds raised first; then the legislature will say, for example, that they want to spend $25 million for alcoholism and drug abuse and 45 percent of that for prevention.

LORNE PHILLIPS, State of Kansas

But in that case you will not get the money. It becomes part of the social health dollar. When advocacy groups and agencies start lining up their handicapped and retarded children and all the other serious health problems for consideration, and we line up our alcoholics, we will not get any dollars.

JANE PATTERSON, State of North Carolina

You will just have to sell your state legislature on prevention.

CHRIS LUBINSKI, U.S. Senate

I think we need to emphasize that taxes are a way of raising money to deal with the problem. As a Senate staff member, I deal primarily with human services. You need not work for the Senate to know that there are fewer funds available to deal with any kind of social problem. Despite the large, recent increase in the alcohol research budget, treatment and prevention funds have been cut severely. It takes money to prepare and print pamphlets, to disseminate information from researchers and physicians in a way that is comprehensible to parents and children. Whether alcohol taxes decrease consumption overall is less important than that we might be successful in getting a 10 or 15 percent set-aside from the funds raised.

We should not set treatment against prevention. We need to treat alcoholics, including youthful alcoholics. We do not want to rob Peter to pay Paul, to take money away from people who are being damaged in order to educate kids. The only way we are going to increase funding substantially on a local or federal level is to generate revenues through user fees. I cannot think of a more appropriate way to do it. If we don't do that, the funds will be taken from another critical area of the federal budget, such as AFDC or food stamps. The issue of excise taxes, rather than being seen mainly as a political means to reduce consumption, should be viewed as a way to raise necessary funds to deal with this problem on all levels.

LORNE PHILLIPS, State of Kansas

In talking about taxes, it is important to think about the trade-offs that might have to be made, which may look good in the short run but do damage in the long run. When we sought new taxes a few years ago in Kansas, it looked good initially because we were historically a dry state. Then we went through a process of licensing private clubs, and that bill included a 10 percent drink tax, which was a real gain. Then we sought a beer tax, and the beer industry wanted certain things in return that the legislature was willing to give them: longer hours, Sunday sales, etc. People in the alcohol field finally backed away from the new tax because what would have to be given up in the way of reduced restrictions on availability was more than we felt we could afford. This is something to look at: Is a tax of so-many-cents-a-drink going to be enough in the long run to pay for what we might end up losing in controls?

DAN BEAUCHAMP, University of North Carolina

I have never understood the alcoholic beverage industry on this point. If I were in the industry, I would encourage this earmarking practice, because it will always lead to a very small tax. A little tax increase raises a lot of money in this field. If we doubled the excise tax and dedicated it all to alcohol-related programs, we would have to put alcoholism treatment centers in everybody's house, we would have so much money to spend. Money for research on alcoholism has gone up dramatically, and the alcoholism constituencies in the states are fairly strong; they are hanging on to their share. I am not so much concerned that we are not going to get enough for them.

CHARLES CRAWFORD, Gallo Winery

Funds need not flow from a government in order to do good. There are other ways. Ernest Gallo has put $3 million into the Ernest Gallo Clinic and Research Center at the University of California, San Francisco, and the San Francisco General Hospital. The research center is trying to develop treatment for withdrawal symptoms, and they are trying to find markers for alcoholism. I think that $3 million will be followed by a lot more money because Mr. Gallo is extremely interested in the question—why do some people become alcoholics and not others? If, through research, a biological marker can be found to identify potential alcoholics before they ever take a drink, we could save billions of dollars and we would not need tax money. Raising excise taxes is not necessarily prevention. Since 1975 the National Institute on Alcohol Abuse and Alcoholism (NIAAA) and other alcoholism groups have spent a lot of money. To raise excise taxes to spend more money in the same direction and not achieve any results could be unfortunate. But if industry itself becomes socially responsible and spends the money, they can get a dollar's worth for every dollar; when governments collect excise taxes they get five cents on every dollar.

BARRY SWEEDLER, National Transportation Safety Board

I do not think we should discount the excise measure. The Swedes, for example, definitely feel that the increasing price of alcohol there has kept consumption down. The Swedish Council for Information on Alcohol and Other Drugs (1982:14) states: "The taxation of alcoholic beverages . . . has also served as perhaps the most powerful instrument of a temperance policy designed to keep consumption within reasonable limits." The user fee analogy has been effective in the drunk-driving area; some states require drunk drivers to pay for their own treatment programs.

FRANK PADAVAN, New York State Senate

In New York State we doubled our fines, and half the money goes back to the counties for education and prevention programs.

MARILYN GOLDWATER, Maryland House of Delegates

I think the key to raising the tax is to get a set-aside. On the federal level that can be done. At the state and county levels, it depends on policy, on what the constitution allows, and on history. Once a few states pass new laws, other states will follow. The first few states have all the difficulty in doing the research necessary to argue effectively for innovative legislation.

JOHN NOBLE, National Institute on Alcohol Abuse and Alcoholism

Tax monies already support treating people who are alcohol abusers and alcoholics. One contribution of identifying tax revenues that deal with consequences is to fuel a trade-off argument: we could stop paying so much for treating the consequences of alcoholism if we could spend some of that money on having fewer people who need such treatment. This cost argument is often made in employee assistance programs. NIAAA can supply baseline data, such as county-level information regarding alcohol consequences.

ROBERT ROSS, State of New York

Everyone would probably agree that, in making policy decisions, it is better to have more research than less. But from a practical point of view, decisions are sometimes made, by a state legislature for example, without the ideal data.

To give a practical example: for a number of years we have been trying to get the New York state tax on alcohol raised, with some portion of that tax dedicated to alcohol prevention and education. Many arguments were used against it: "We don't have enough data, we don't know this, we don't know that." Suddenly we had a $1.8 billion gap in the budget, and this year a $32 million increase in the tax on alcoholic beverages was passed. But it was passed without answering such questions as: On what beverages will it be placed? What is it going to be used for? Is it only going to be general revenue or is it going to be general revenue plus usage for prevention activities? Are we going to attempt to evaluate the impact on consumption?

It may not have been a bad decision in terms of revenue, but a wonderful opportunity was lost when the decision was made to increase the tax on alcohol by $32 million and do nothing on those issues, instead of raising it $36 million and putting $4 million more into the prevention system. One could not say that the beverage patrons could accept a $32 million increase but not a $36 million increase, without going out of state for purchase and consumption. There is no rational argument that anything more than $32 million would have been overbearing. The legislature made that decision without benefit of a convenient body of information that said: "If and when you get ready to pass this increase, here are the questions that you should address, here are the kinds of things you should do." They have heard all the arguments individually over a period of time from the Division on Alcoholism and Alcohol Abuse and other people who are interested in alcoholism issues in New York, but they did not have a nice compact 8- or 10-page statement with appropriate references that said, "If you are going to change policy, here is what you ought to do, here are the people you ought to consult."

These kinds of opportunities are very frustrating, because the tax may not be changed again in the near future. We have all lost an opportunity, and I do not think anyone has gained anything on the other side—it was done for expediency and everyone understood that. But with the right kind of support, some sort of prevention study to see what the impact would be could easily have been provided for.

HENRY KING, United States Brewers Association

That example is not unique. I have directed the legislative lobbying activities of the brewing industry for 21 years, and I cannot recall many instances of states raising the tax on alcohol in which either our opponents' or our arguments were fully considered on their merits. We have all done the best for our constituencies according to what we believed was our proper role, but it always comes down to economic budget considerations and the interplay of political forces. That is the way the process works. We live in a political environment in which deals go on in a legislature that have nothing to do with the ultimate merits of an issue.

The industry, incidentally, is not at all opposed to many things that have been suggested over the years; for example, the industry supports the interim recommendations of the Presidential Commission on Drunk Driving and is actively trying to generate legislative support at the state level. I have sat for 14 months on the Presidential Commission on Drunk Driving and have seen no data that would give me a conscientious reason to vote against a 21-year-old minimum purchase age, for example.

I find this conference extremely helpful, to talk to one another directly. I would have been afraid to sit across the table from someone who suggested that we should limit the number of licenses. Maybe we should, but we need a lot more research, information, and dialogue.

BEN MASON, Adolph Coors Company

I have some concern that we may be on the wrong track. Let me give you an analogy. I worked in education policy for a number of years and saw educators seduced into addressing tax policy issues at the local level, becoming terribly embroiled in issues of equal access, equal opportunities, equal burdens, almost to the exclusion of focusing on the purposes of education. Now we articulate rather well the tax policy issues related to education, though decisions are made to a great extent as Henry King described. However, we do not focus very well on what we expect education to accomplish. As a person interested in primary prevention, I am concerned that the debates over tax policy at the state level are long, terribly complicated, and politically brutal, and dilute the focus of what we want out of primary prevention programs. I do not think there is enough collective wisdom at this conference or most others to be persuasive in the area of tax policy, whereas we could be persuasive in drawing conclusions about primary prevention program accomplishments.

Certainly we should develop a variety of approaches to prevention. But given the amount of data we have about tax policy, I am concerned that we not get sidetracked by something that takes energies away from the real objective of reducing the harmful effects of abuse.

SHEILA BLUME, National Council on Alcoholism

I am not moved by the argument that we should not talk about taxes because we should talk about something else. It seems to me that prevention policy is too often based on "either/or." "If you are interested in school education, then you cannot possibly talk about taxes." Or "if you are training servers then you are forgetting about the people who are drinking at home." There is no single way to take hold of everything at once. If we ever develop a rational prevention policy, it will have hundreds of items in it, some more and some less effective, but they will all have to be done.

4 Engaging the Business Sector

A NEW DIRECTION IN ALCOHOL POLICY: COMPREHENSIVE SERVER INTERVENTION

James F. Mosher, Medical Research Institute of San Francisco

Perhaps the most significant contribution made by the report *Alcohol and Public Policy: Beyond the Shadow of Prohibition* (Moore and Gerstein, 1981) is its delineation of new, alternative strategies for preventing alcohol-related problems. These strategies fall under three general categories: (1) regulation of the supply of alcohol; (2) legal, educational, training, and mass media interventions aimed at changing harmful consumer drinking practices; and (3) environmental interventions. These approaches complement traditional individualized treatment and prevention programs by addressing alcohol-related problems at a community and societal level.

The panel noted, but perhaps without sufficient emphasis, that the design and implementation of prevention policies require a comprehensive approach that coordinates the three types of interventions. As stated in the report's conclusion (p. 116):

We are convinced that the regulation of supply, legal and pedagogical approaches to drinking practices, and interventions in the environment mediating between drinking and certain of its consequences, represent valid approaches with promise for sustained improvement. Each detailed element will fail or succeed only as it is implemented properly and thoroughly; tactics that are undertaken as

57

part of a broad and coordinated approach are more likely to be effective than ones undertaken in isolation.

This is a critical point for the discussion of prevention-oriented regulations of the supply of alcoholic beverages. As the panel documents, current research offers only modest support for the proposition that supply regulations other than taxation and minimum-age drinking laws have a positive effect on the incidence of alcohol-related problems (p. 78):

The effects of merchandising practices, outlet density, civil liability for servers, and so forth have not been established with reliability, in part because these control mechanisms are intrinsically very difficult to study. It is possible but as yet hypothetical that the cumulative effect of a number of changes in these areas of regulation has been substantial.

Server intervention programs provide a case study on the need for a comprehensive approach to supply-oriented prevention programming, one that encompasses several complementary intervention strategies. Server intervention refers to the actions taken by servers of alcoholic beverages to reduce the likelihood that those being served will harm themselves or others. Servers include commercial vendors (persons or entities licensed to sell alcoholic beverages and their employees) and their noncommercial counterparts (social hosts and others such as fraternities and employers, who provide alcohol to specific groups in the course of special events). Server intervention, then, refers primarily to the regulation of the supply of alcoholic beverages by restricting the manner in which alcohol is made available for consumption. Yet the key to a successful server intervention program is the development and implementation of a multifaceted approach that includes legal and environmental interventions as well as training programs for servers.

I would like to introduce the various elements of such a comprehensive program, describe existing programs, evaluate their strengths and weaknesses, and recommend future agendas for program development, including research priorities. (For more thorough discussions of these topics, see Mosher, 1979, 1982, 1983b.)

The Key Components of Server Intervention Programs

As previously noted, server intervention programs can be divided conceptually into three basic components: training, environmental, and legal. Strategies directed at drinkers to enlist their acceptance of preventive actions taken by servers (mass media appeals, legal sanctions, educational programs, etc.—the pedagogical approach to prevention described by the panel), could be considered a fourth, complementary component. It is not discussed here, as it does not represent a central aspect of server intervention programs. The training component consists of educational programs directed at those who serve alcoholic beverages (either commercial servers or social hosts) and those who manage commercial alcohol outlets. The programs are designed to teach servers how to reduce the risk of intoxication among those who are served ("patrons" or "guests") and to prevent patrons or guests who do become intoxicated from causing harm to themselves or others. Many curricula have been developed throughout the country and typically include sessions on the effects of alcohol on the body; signs of intoxication; legal responsibilities of servers; methods for cutting off service to intoxicated patrons; methods for handling intoxicated patrons; management practices that support training recommendations; and alcoholism treatment.

The environmental component involves where alcohol is being served and its relationship to other alcohol outlets; the location's interior and exterior design; and its relationship to transportation factilities, either public or private. These factors have been identified and researched only sporadically, although they are occasionally discussed as part of server training programs or as an overall prevention strategy for reducing drunk driving.

The legal component consists of three distinct bodies of state and local law. First, state and local regulation of commercial alcohol outlets (usually found in state and local alcoholic beverage control [ABC] codes) determine the ground rules by which such businesses operate— who may sell, to whom and in what circumstances and locations, and what business practices must be followed. Second, many (but not all) states impose dram shop (civil) liability on commercial servers of alcohol (and, in some cases, social hosts) if they serve obviously intoxicated or underage persons who subsequently cause harm to themselves or others. Finally, states set criminal sanctions on certain server practices (usually applicable to both commercial and noncommercial servers), most of which are also included in civil liability and ABC codes. Prohibitions on service to underage and obviously intoxicated persons are the most typical criminal provisions relevant to server intervention programs.

Existing Server Intervention Programs

Server intervention programs have been instituted on a limited, experimental basis in several states during the last five years. In general the programs have focused on the training component, targeted commercial establishments, developed innovative curricula, and been well received by licensees and their employees. The brief description below of four existing server intervention programs offers a sampling of program designs now being implemented.

Other programs exist in numerous sites, most of which rely primarily on a training or educational curriculum aimed at servers. For example, the New York State Division of Alcoholism and Alcohol Abuse is conducting educational seminars for commercial servers in cooperation with the New York State Restaurant Association; Mothers Against Drunk Drivers has instituted a similar seminar series in California, as has the Health Education Foundation in Washington, D.C. The S & A Restaurant Corporation has an in-house server training program used in its restaurants throughout the country.

The California DUI Project   The first comprehensive server training program, and the one most thoroughly studied, was conducted by the California ABC Department from 1977 to 1980. A detailed study was written in 1979 discussing the history and components of the program and offering recommendations for its continuation (Mosher and Wallack, 1979a). The DUI (driving under the influence) project had several innovative features. First, licenses were identified by the use of DUI arrest forms. Law enforcement personnel asked all DUI arrestees to indicate the location of their last drink. All licensees identified were tabulated, and if one location was listed three or more times ABC staff would contact the licensee and offer a training course. Participation was voluntary; after some initial suspicion, most licensees contacted did participate. In fact, by the end of the first year, after 540 training courses involving 5,720 server personnel, more requests for training were being received than could be conducted. In the second year, the course was conducted for those requesting it without use of the identification process.

The DUI project developed an innovative set of training materials which covered: (1) how to anticipate intoxicated patrons; (2) factors affecting intoxication; (3) effects of intoxication; (4) problems and rationalizations in cutting off service; (5) suggestions for when to cut off service; (6) suggestions for how to cut off service; (7) what to do after cutting off service; (8) myths about alcohol; (9) the drinking capacities of people by weight; (10) potentially effective house policies.

Finally, the project included training sessions for the trainers. ABC personnel were hired as trainers, most of whom had no previous experience in conducting educational workshops. Mosher and Wallack found that this design had both strengths and weaknesses. On one hand, it increased the communication between licensees and ABC field staff, which had many indirect benefits. In addition, the experience greatly broadened the interests and knowledge of the ABC trainers, thus responding to an identified problem in ABC policies (see Medicine in the Public Interest, 1979). On the other hand, the trainers lacked many of the skills necessary for conducting training sessions, and because of limited funding full-time efforts were not possible.

Mosher and Wallack offered several recommendations, including integrating more effectively the enforcement and other legal aspects of the program, redesigning the training sessions, and conducting follow-ups. Despite its weaknesses, the DUI project offers an interesting and important first step in developing server intervention programs.

The Madison, Wisconsin, Training Program On 1 August 1981 Madison, Wisconsin, enacted a local ordinance requiring that all commercial servers of alcohol participate in a Bartender Alcohol Awareness Training Program as a condition of obtaining a local license. A local technical education organization has conducted the mandated training sessions pursuant to the local ordinance. The four sessions of training cover four major topics: city ordinances and state statutes; drunk driving laws and blood alcohol content; the effects of alcohol and other drugs and facts on alcoholism and treatment programs; and human relations, marketing, and responsibilities (Shold and Morgan, 1982). Shold and Morgan report that the program has gained much support from community enforcement personnel, alcohol-related programs, and community tavern leagues and associations. Pre- and post-test evaluations were conducted to determine whether those trained had gained an understanding of the training materials. The results showed very high rates of comprehension and new knowledge. No evaluation has been conducted on the implementation of the training material or the outcome of implementation. Nevertheless, the Madison program is unique in this country in its use of the legal component.

The Massachusetts Server Training and Intervention Program The efforts of a single educator have resulted in a server training and intervention program in Massachusetts (Peters, 1982). Peters has developed a curriculum focusing on the prevention role of bartenders. The materials include information on alcohol and on bartenders' roles in policing, counseling, and supervising patrons. Peters has supplemented his training efforts with legislative initiatives. Working throughout one Massachusetts city, he has succeeded in implementing changes in bar practices (including fewer happy hours, citywide training sessions, shifts in advertising, and more active cutting off of intoxicated patrons) using both legal ordinances and voluntary compliance. Statewide legislation has been introduced to require server training as a condition of licensing. Although this is a promising program, very little has been written describing these activities, and no evaluation has been conducted.

The Minnesota Community Program for Server Intervention   The University of Minnesota's Office of Alcohol and Other Drug Abuse Programming is developing a community-based prevention program for alcohol problems that has as one component server intervention strategies (Schaefer, 1982). Unlike the other programs reviewed here, the Minnesota program has not relied primarily on training sessions. Licensees have been contacted on individual and group bases, and various intervention techniques have been promoted. The program emphasizes voluntary action, including licensee-sponsored training sessions for employees (Schaefer, 1982). Legal strategies have also been proposed in one locality, and in an innovative approach, insurance companies have been contacted with an eye to possible reforms in dram shop liability policies.

Weaknesses of Current Programs

These programs represent a significant step in server intervention policy—they are practical efforts to incorporate commercial alcohol establishments into a prevention effort. There are four major weaknesses in their design, however, which must be addressed if effective programs are to be developed.

First, most existing programs emphasize voluntary training of commercial servers without regard to environmental factors affecting server practices. For example, none of the programs provides any assessment of outlet design on servers' practices and patrons' drinking patterns. Many training curricula emphasize that servers should make unobtrusive and comprehensive observations of patrons' activities. Yet the outlet may be designed such that adequate patron observation is difficult or impossible. Recent research suggests that drinking settings have an important impact on drinking behavior (e.g., Rosenbluth et al., 1978; Skog, 1979; Schaefer, 1981). Such variables as crowdedness, noise, availability of nonalcoholic beverages and food and of nondrinking activities that promote sociability may substantially reduce the need for interventions by bartenders and other employees. Voluntary training sessions for outlet personnel will have little impact on these factors.

Also overlooked in the environmental component is the issue of location. Most importantly, what is the relationship of the outlet to transportation facilities? An effective server intervention program must be attentive to how patrons are traveling to and from the premises. Adequate alternatives to private automobiles are needed in case a patron becomes inebriated. Recent efforts have been made in some locales to provide free taxi, minibus, or public transportation services during peak drinking times such as holiday weekends. Such programs may provide a model for alternative transportation plans on a regular basis. At a minimum, outlets should develop a regular taxi program, ensuring immediate responses to requests for taxi service and regular reliance on taxis when a patron becomes intoxicated. A training course that suggests the use of taxis will have little impact if taxis are slow to respond or are unavailable.

A second weakness of many (but not all) current programs, suggested by the first, is their relative inattention to the role of management. There is a tendency to focus merely on those in the front line—bartenders, cocktail waitresses, and other employees actually in contact with the establishment's customers. An effective intervention program, however, may require a number of reforms in management practices, including such variables as the number of employees on the job, the number of patrons allowed on the premises, the interior design, the commitment to alternative forms of transportation, the hours of operation, the use of promotional techniques, etc. Programs must not only address these issues in their training curricula, but they must also develop formats and approaches that will enlist management's commitment to a comprehensive approach.

Third, current programs underutilize the legal levers available for their implementation. The Madison program, which was instituted with a local ordinance requiring server training as a condition of operating a commercial establishment, provides a good example of the potential role of law in server intervention programs. But a much greater complementary role is needed. ABC codes establish the basic guidelines for server practices and license location and can, in conjunction with local regulations, provide a basis for implementing both the training and environmental aspects of a server intervention program. In addition to requiring server training, ABC codes should set standards for server and management practices that complement the training materials and should incorporate preventive environmental standards. For example, special license restrictions can be placed on premises that rely heavily on private auto travel (e.g., most sports stadiums) or that are targeted by those under the legal drinking age for purchases (e.g., convenience stores). Licenses can be denied if the proposed location is ill-advised due to traffic patterns or if the proposed manner of sale tends to associate drinking with driving (e.g., licenses at gas stations).

Such reforms require a major shift in current ABC policies and priorities. As a 1979 study conducted by Medicine in the Public Interest found, ABC laws lack a preventive focus and fail to define a coordinated, effective control system. In addition, ABC policy makers tend to have an extremely narrow vision of the role of ABC policies and do not coordinate their activities with other governmental officials charged with preventing alcohol-related problems.

The role of the dram shop liability statutes and court case decisions, additional legal levers for implementing server intervention programs, has also been ignored. Commercial servers in more than 25 states may be held civilly liable for injuries caused by their intoxicated patrons (see Mosher, 1979, for a review). Unfortunately, current legal procedures have severely limited the potential impact of this legal doctrine on server intervention programs. First, the standard used for determining whether a commercial server should be found negligent—whether the server has given alcohol to an "obviously intoxicated person"—is too vague. It does not offer practical guidance to the server for avoiding liability and is subject to adverse interpretations by juries, who tend to sympathize with victims. Second, insurance company policies often favor settlement of unjustified claims, making up the expenditures by increasing insurance premium rates. These factors combine to reduce a licensee's incentive to reform their server practices in order to avoid liability, as even the most responsible licensee is in danger of unjustified but successful legal actions. Instead, licensees often rely on insurance coverage for protection from financial harm, which converts dram shop laws into imperfect victim-compensation mechanisms (see Mosher, 1979, for a comprehensive analysis of current dram shop policies).

These limitations could be corrected if liability were made contingent on a licensee's decision to take reasonable steps to prevent injuries to third parties. For example, a server who institutes a training program for employees, implements management practices that encourage compliance, and is attentive to environmental variables such as alternative transportation for intoxicated patrons could be protected as a matter of law from dram shop suits, assuming he or she could prove that the procedures were followed on a given occasion. Such a legal reform would provide a strong financial incentive for licensees to institute an effective server intervention program, particularly if insurance companies encourage action by basing their premiums on the existence of preventive policies. (For further discussion of the legal reform, see

Mosher, 1979, and Stepnick, 1983. Stepnick analyzes the economic costs and benefits of a "responsible practices" defense to dram shop suits, concluding that there would be a significant economic benefit to society. The North Carolina legislature is now considering a bill that would institute a "responsible practices" law in that state; see Governor's Task Force on Drunken Drivers, 1982.)

Finally, the current server intervention programs have not conducted adequate evaluations. Both the California and the Madison programs did conduct pre- and post-tests to determine the comprehension of training materials. However, no program has attempted to determine whether the training materials have actually been implemented and, if so, what their impact is on patrons' drinking behavior. In the absence of such evaluations, the suggested practices remain in the realm of conjecture and common sense. As stated in the panel's report (p. 76): "At this time, in the absence of research data, the effectiveness of [dram shop] laws or variations therein is entirely a matter of anecdote, *a priori* speculation, and common sense argument."

Future Agendas

The discussion of the weaknesses of current programs provides the basis for setting future agendas, which should focus on research and evaluations.

Experimental Training Programs   Experimental programs are needed that offer the opportunity to evaluate the difficulties of implementing particular server interventions and their impact once implemented. Settings such as military bases, college campuses, and other isolated locations should be chosen initially to minimize the number of potentially confounding variables, and a variety of outcome and process measures, including statistical and observational data, should be used. Attention should be given both to the process of implementation as well as the outcome. As such evaluations are completed, programs can be redesigned and replicated in settings that are more difficult to evaluate.

The programs should be limited, at least initially, to commercial settings. There are several reasons for such a priority. First, most dram shop laws and ABC regulations are themselves limited to licensed vendors and are not applicable to social hosts and other noncommercial servers. Second, because they are in the business of selling alcoholic beverages, commercial vendors have a special responsibility, reflected in existing laws and regulations, to take reasonable precautions in the operation of their businesses to protect the public from harm. Such business responsibilities are common to other professions offering services to the public; the primary debate should not be the existence of that responsibility but rather its scope. Third, the limited available research suggests that a large portion of drunk drivers depart from commercial establishments. A 1973 report of a national roadside breath-testing survey found that 44 percent of those tested with blood alcohol levels of .10 or more were driving to, from, or between public eating and drinking places (Wolfe, 1974). Data from interviews of those arrested for drunk driving suggest similar findings (Yoder, 1975; Mosher and Wallack, 1979a). Finally, because server intervention is at an experimental stage, only a limited portion of the total spectrum of servers should be included in initial programs, research, and evaluations. Commercial establishments offer good settings for the conduct of research and evaluations; once particular commercial interventions are identified as effective, one can begin designing interventions for noncommercial settings, thus creating a ripple effect.

Legal Research   For server intervention programs to be effective, they need a comprehensive legal component. Current legal research is inadequate to fulfill this task. Provisions affecting server practices found in ABC statutes and regulations need to be catalogued and analyzed, and dram shop cases need to be researched to determine the types of situations most likely to lead to legal actions. As discussed in Mosher (1983b), existing research does not include any analyses of dram shop court cases other than those reaching the appeals court level. As a result there is no information on the prevalence of dram shop cases, their outcomes, the types of individuals and establishments involved, and the impact of insurance company practices.

Environmental Research   Policy decisions at state ABC departments seldom reflect the number or location of outlets or their interior and exterior design. Yet what little research exists suggests that these factors could be the primary guide for community and ABC licensing and enforcement decisions (see Wittman, 1980, 1982). Research should also include studies on the impact of various types of alcohol outlets (e.g., stadiums, nightclubs, gas stations, etc.) on drinking problems and on the drinking locations of drinking drivers. Findings should be used to inform and modify management and server training programs.

Model Legislation   Model ABC laws and dram shop legislation should be drafted and implemented on the basis of findings from research and evaluation. The impact of such legislation should be assessed as various provisions are enacted using a "natural experiment" methodology similar to that used in minimum-age drinking studies (e.g., Wagenaar, 1982).

Conclusion

Server intervention has received considerable public attention in the past two years, and several programs have come into existence during that time. Groups recommending implementation of at least some aspect of server intervention programs include the Presidential Task Force on Drunk Driving, Mothers Against Drunk Drivers, the National Highway Traffic Safety Administration, several state task forces on drunk driving, and numerous scholars (e.g., Mosher, 1979; Beauchamp, 1980; Bonnie, 1981; Reed, 1981). Legal interventions are now being considered in several states, including Connecticut, Massachusetts, California, South Dakota, and North Carolina. Industry groups have become interested in developing in-house programs, and several such programs are now in place in various locales (see, e.g., Peters, 1982; Schaefer, 1982; Waring and Spier, 1982). Even the Health Education Foundation, an organization often opposed to legal interventions as a means to prevent alcohol-related problems, is developing a server training curriculum and has recommended dram shop laws as a means for implementation.

As support for server intervention spreads, the demand for additional programs will undoubtedly increase. This enthusiasm needs to be tempered to reflect the major tasks that must be completed before effective programs are possible. State ABC departments, insurance companies, enforcement agencies, private industry, citizen support groups, researchers, evaluators, educational specialists, and local community organizations need to focus on the difficult research and implementation problems and to coordinate their activities. The federal government, through the National Institute on Alcohol Abuse and Alcoholism (NIAAA), needs to take the lead in this process, providing financial resources for the necessary research and evaluation studies, offering technical assistance to interested groups, acting as an information clearinghouse, and ensuring that duplication of effort is minimized.

Server intervention programs offer strong support for two of the panel's major conclusions—that control of the supply of alcoholic beverages is one viable strategy for preventing drinking problems, and that comprehensive programs encompassing a variety of interventions are needed. The promise embodied in the panel's report, however, can become a reality only if there is both careful planning by policy makers and a strong commitment for change among the many affected groups and individuals in our society.

THE ROLE OF THE STATE ALCOHOL AUTHORITY

JOHN F. VASALLO, JR., State of New Jersey

The main role of state liquor administrators and ABC boards, commissions, divisions, etc., is to apply and enforce the law. Unfortunately most of us are limited in what we can do because of budget restrictions; none of us has enough money. In New Jersey I have only 15 undercover agents to handle almost 8 million people, and funds are even being cut from that. We cannot attract people to this field with the monies that can be paid.

The approach we have to take is to support good practice in the industry that supplies, wholesales, and serves alcoholic beverages. We cannot regulate and control the industry to such a degree that no abuses flow from it. The primary responsibility of a regulator is to ensure that the regulations do not harm those who are regulated. Of course the welfare of the entire people is the underlying reason for any government regulation at all. A state regulator must be concerned with the public interest, but the rights of those who are regulated must be balanced with it. Rules must be set down for the growth and welfare of the industry as well as the benefit of the general public. Where they conflict, the needs of the general public must come first.

A good analogy: to the alcohol beverage industry, the role of a state administrator is like that of a father. A father guides and sets rules to ensure a child's greatest growth and achievement of potential within the confines of those rules and at the same time to provide a benefit to society as a whole. The same applies to regulating the alcohol beverage industry. Guidelines may be set down, but if they are too stringent, licensees will find ways to get around them. Rules and regulations must be realistic. Because those regulated sometimes get out of line, it is necessary to discipline them, much as it is necessary to discipline a child. It is done, however, with the intent of bringing them back into line and correcting them rather than punishing them, as a stable alcohol beverage industry is the ultimate goal. The fatherly role consists of trying to guide the licensees along the lines that the legislature has set down, protecting them, promoting their interests, but at the same time paddling their backsides when they get out of hand. That may sound a little facetious or a little farfetched, but that is the job that has to be done.

I consider myself fortunate to regulate the system of distribution in New Jersey because that system is quite limited. Since licensees have to obtain consumption licenses with full privileges for the sale of all types of alcoholic beverages, and those licenses are limited according to the population of municipalities, availability of beer and wine in restaurants or food stores is not widespread. Some food stores have purchased retail consumption licenses, but they must have their beer/wine/liquor department completely separated from the general shelves of the supermarket.

One of the primary reasons that the system in New Jersey has worked very well and should continue to work well is that the licensees have such a large investment. Generally it costs quite a bit to purchase a liquor license, and there is a sizable annual fee. There is also equity in the license; it can be resold for a substantially appreciated sum. Licensees do not want to risk losing this investment. Their lives and businesses are centered around their license; it is one of their most valuable assets and will be protected. Consequently they take more precautions than would otherwise be expected in order to keep that license from being threatened.

In other states outlets that sell only beer and wine, whether by the drink or by the bottle, are primarily in the restaurant or food business. The beer and wine activity is secondary and does not matter as much to them; it is only a small part of their profits. If the privilege is lost, the business is not lost. Consequently there is not as great an interest in devoting the time and effort necessary to ensure that violations do not occur and that the distribution of alcohol takes place properly and lawfully.

Using this paternalistic approach, we try to create a certain atmosphere through regulations and enforcement. We try to get the licensees to take pride in what they are doing, to take precautions, to value their license and privilege, to respect it, and to respect what they are adding to the economy. These licensees are very important to the economy of the state. A tremendous number of people are employed as either a direct or an indirect result of alcoholic beverage activity. Many restaurants would not be able to offer employment to as many waiters and waitresses if they did not serve alcoholic beverages: the sale of alcoholic beverages can be a high gross-profit item, which can absorb the costs of serving food and providing an enjoyable atmosphere. It is also important to tourism; in addition, many people in New Jersey are employed in the glass bottle industry, on which the alcohol beverage industry depends.

The overall economic effect of the industry is great; therefore we don't want to adversely affect the situation and cause unemployment or other hardships to the general public. In other words, in regulating alcoholic beverages, especially when trying to control their supply and distribution, we must keep in mind that cutting down the quantity is going to have many adverse effects. It is thus necessary to view the broad picture.

Some negative serving practices occur among those who have not been in the industry for long. The fight for the dollar leads to practices such as "two drinks for the price of one." I notice this practice throughout the country, but the New Jersey Administrative Code (13:2-23-16(a)2) prohibits giving anything of value conditioned on the purchase of an alcoholic beverage, and on the basis of this regulation I do not allow two-for-one. Certain licensees do not like this. They are permitted happy hour specials with drinks at half-price, but selling drinks at half-price could cut down on total cash flow since certain people may order only one drink. These licensees do not want to diminish their revenue; they would rather pour a few more ounces of alcohol. Our feeling, however, is that an enticement must be a genuine bargain and not something disguised. A person should not have to be served a double amount of alcohol in order to get the benefit of the "bargain."

The big difficulty with two-for-one and other specials that increase the amount of consumption is that the tolerance or capacity of the patron is not known at the time of serving the drink. By the time the person finishes two drinks, that tolerance level may have been passed, even though it might not be a presumptive intoxication level when measuring blood alcohol content. The blood alcohol level at which people feel the effects of alcoholic beverages varies, and the tolerance of alcoholics is generally much higher than that of nondrinkers or occasional social drinkers. This is also why we do not condone the practice of supplying more than one drink at a time. This type of thing leads to alcohol problems.

I am also critical of happy hour promotions that run far longer than an hour, sometimes an entire day: I saw a sign in one restaurant that read: "Happy Hours: Sunday through Saturday." Placing controls on these practices or trying to get licensees to curtail these practices voluntarily is an effective way of regulating the supply of alcohol. It is much better to obtain voluntary cooperation from licensees than to try to force them to do something they do not want to do. Coercion fosters attempts to get around the regulation. For example, when we took initial steps with certain licensees to curtail two-for-one practices, rather than giving two drinks in two glasses, they doubled the size of the glass during the time of the promotion. Patrons then did not realize how much alcohol they were getting.

Another approach that is sometimes suggested is controlling the amount of alcohol that may be put in a shot, but this is really not satisfactory, as alcohol comes in different proofs. That strategy would require regulating the size of the shot in proportion to the volume of alcoholic content.

Another development involves the type of alcohol available. The laws we work with in many cases go back to the 1930s, and they do not cover all present circumstances. I have noticed recently on the shelves a 190-proof grain alcohol, sold in small bottles as miniatures. If we cannot encourage licensees to get rid of these voluntarily, then we will take other steps to get rid of them.

Educational and instructional programs for licensees can be very effective, but I feel strongly that they can only be successful on a voluntary level. Attempts at instruction of licensees in New Jersey on a voluntary basis have been somewhat successful. I think there is an interest on the part of licensees who are serious about their business and have some stake in learning what they can do to avoid problems. Licensees are keenly aware of these problems, especially if they are subject to dram shop liability.

THE CORPORATE ROLE IN PREVENTING ALCOHOL ABUSE

ROGER THOMSON, S & A Restaurant Corporation

My firm, the S & A Restaurant Corporation, has approximately 300 licensed restaurants nationwide. Some are in the state of New Jersey, from where John Vassallo—my "father," whom I have just met—hails, and where we have indeed been paddled. We are as concerned as everyone else about people dying on the roads, and we are trying to take an active stance to deal effectively with this situation. We are spending a great deal of time, money, and effort to educate our employees *and* our patrons on the sharing of responsibility. We do not force anyone to enter our restaurants; but once they do, we have a responsibility to attempt to see that they do not get intoxicated. This does not, however, absolve patrons of *their* responsibility not to get intoxicated. Responsibility should be a shared burden and that concept should carry over to dram shop liability, which is a complex field.

Nationwide we have posted notices in some of our restaurants to remind our customers that they have a responsibility, and we will refuse to serve them if we think they are not taking this responsibility. We also have blood alcohol content charts posted in some restrooms and telephone booths. If we think that somebody may be drinking too much, we may serve them protein- and fat-rich foods that absorb alcohol more quickly. We may also place on our new menus a nonalcoholic beverage section that receives top billing. We have game areas that allow people to feel that they do not have to sit and drink first to enjoy a meal, and we are initiating other diversions for people who choose not to drink alcohol. Where we have been able to strike deals with taxi companies, our restaurants have a hot line to the taxi company: Just pick up the phone, which is a direct line, and we pay for the cab to take home a patron who has had too much to drink.

To educate our staff, we invite the local police and the local alcohol councils to speak to our employees frequently. In our newspaper, which goes to all our restaurants, there is often an article on some aspect of alcohol. We help our employees recognize the signs of intoxication and we give them support to cut an intoxicated person off. On the community level, we funnel money into various school systems to produce posters on responsibility and alcohol. We work with Mothers Against Drunk Drivers and other groups on various local issues. We are trying to be responsible.

I think the vast majority of restaurants is very concerned about this situation and is trying to be responsive to the problems. Our efforts to be responsive should be shared by those who patronize our facilities, and all reasonable steps should be taken to ensure this sharing of responsibility.

COMMENTS ON THE INTERSECTION OF PUBLIC AND PRIVATE SECTORS

HENRY KING, United States Brewers Association

There is a restaurant in Washington named Mel Krupin's, a famous political and press hangout, which will not permit patrons to get intoxicated. They know how much you drink and they just stop you. I have been eating there 4 nights a week for 10 years, and I have never seen an intoxicated person in the restaurant, though I have seen people stopped from coming in. This place has a great reputation for being aware of the problem. It does not put signs in the men's room saying, "Drink in moderation." The employees are trained, and you cannot get in without being observed.

ROBERT REYNOLDS, County of San Diego

The issue here is not whether isolated restaurateurs have these policies but whether as a matter of public policy this kind of training should be a prerequisite for licensing. Consumer action might be effective in developing server training programs in many more establishments that serve alcoholic beverages.

SHEILA BLUME, National Council on Alcoholism

In New York State, the Division of Alcoholism and Alcohol Abuse has started a pilot program of bartender and server training. The division's executive deputy, counsel, and executive assistant met with the restaurant owners' representatives, who identified escalating liability insurance as one of their biggest problems. By putting the two groups' resources together, a training package was developed, including videotaped scenes of bartenders turning intoxicated patrons away gently and other simulations of actual situations. By the time the first pilot was launched, both the tavern owners and the Division of Alcoholism were enthusiastic about it. The strategy was finding a common interest between the restaurant owners and the Division of Alcoholism. The common goal is based on the economic liability to which the restaurant owners were subject, not due to a change in social values, but to smart lawyers who were suing them and to what they were consequently paying for insurance coverage. The strategy is to do something positive, rather than wait to repair damage after the fact. I do not think it is a matter of people being less tolerant of drunkenness, but one of economic interest.

ROBERT ROSS, State of New York

The Division of Alcoholism is now planning 15 local training sessions, reaching approximately 1,000 people, for which the restaurant owners will pay while our division provides the expertise and staffing. We will train the employees, not just the owners, who work in member restaurants of the state association; it is not costing the state anything extra. The restaurant people, who come voluntarily, see the training as a big plus because they would otherwise have to purchase it at much greater cost. From our point of view the training is a big plus because it establishes a working relationship with an industry surrounded by a lot of friction due to regulations, increased taxes, drunk-driving law changes, etc. This is an isolated instance of cooperation in the midst of a battle between the industry and the state government.

HENRY KING, United States Brewers Association

Mothers Against Drunk Drivers, in cooperation with the Tavern and Restaurant Owners in Sacramento, has an ongoing educational program, as does the University of Massachusetts. Morris Chafetz at the Health Education Foundation is developing a program. The Presidential Commission on Drunk Driving is making very strong recommendations that the industry conduct educational programs for owners and employees; that report will be a stimulus for the industry and other groups. We are just at the threshold. New York was one of the first. I think that in two to three years this will be a national program with some continuity to it.

GEORGE HACKER, Center for Science in the Public Interest

What is the relative amount of drinking that occurs at home or in private settings versus the amount that occurs at public gatherings like sports events or in public taverns and restaurants, where professional servers control the situation? To the extent that we develop policies aimed at limiting excessive drinking in public settings, do we run the risk of ignoring the broader prevention policies that will affect people who drink in their own homes and other private settings?

HENRY KING, United States Brewers Association

Less than 40 percent of beer is consumed in taverns and restaurants. There is some—we do not know how much—illegal consumption of beer by those under legal age. It would be safe to say that probably 65 percent of the beer is consumed either in the home or in a place other than a tavern.

LARRY STEWART, Caucus of Producers, Writers, and Directors

If we could find data showing that too many alcohol-related accidents happened to people leaving stadiums, arenas, etc., then it would be a problem for the private sector, the various leagues, to solve, perhaps by exerting efforts to "cool it," to curtail consumption in fourth quarters, ninth innings, etc.

HENRY KING, United States Brewers Association

The brewing industry supports such an effort. We have had terribly unruly situations, for example, with 10-cent-beer nights at baseball games. It does not enhance the image of the brewing industry to have people brawling and throwing things at ballplayers. It certainly does not make for moderation and intelligent use. There should be some controls. In some cities and some areas that have controls, they do not have those kinds of violent actions. The brewers have made overtures to these athletic groups. If other constituent groups would join in and raise the roof, we could get more attention.

JAMES F. MOSHER, Medical Research Institute of San Francisco

Even though most of the beer—in fact most of the alcohol in all forms—is consumed beyond the purview of professional servers, a program or policy to change servers' behavior is an important general preventive measure for two reasons: the proportion of drinking overseen, while not the majority in terms of volume, is quite substantial; and serving practices in private settings will inevitably be affected both by the public example of concern set by new professional practices and by the diffusion of experience gained by employees, trainers, and researchers into the common body of knowledge and custom.

JEFFREY E. HARRIS, Massachusetts Institute of Technology

General interest in life-style change and disease prevention has been growing in the population and the modern American corporation. There seems to be an enormous demand for life-style–related programs, such as fitness and exercise programs, which have the additional advantage of being tax-exempt fringe benefits. The prevention of alcohol abuse is an area in which modern corporations must become increasingly interested. According to the federal Rehabilitation Act, a company cannot simply fire someone who comes in drunk; it has to take remedial action. This is a particular gap that needs to be filled.

LARRY STEWART, Caucus of Producers, Writers, and Directors

In the television and motion picture industries, eight major studios have opened facilities on their lots for Alcoholics Anonymous (AA) meetings, collateral Al-Anon meetings, and the like. The same studios are now financing a halfway house for motion picture and television employees, be they carpenters or executives. That new thrust has occurred over the last few years. AA involvement has become a bulletin board item in those studios; every employee who checks out by the clock or checks job-related situations on bulletin boards is aware that those facilities are open and help is available within the studio system.

KEITH SCHUCHARD, Parental Resource Institute for Drug Education

The Georgia Power Company is educating every member of the company, from janitors to the chairman of the board, on the health consequences of alcohol and drug abuse. The company is trying to help everyone understand the content of advertising and to appeal to them as intelligent citizens—as parents, young people, friends, etc.—to make use of the employee counseling resources. This program is not focusing just on illness or on Georgia Power's concern about safety in its nuclear power plants; the company is calling on its employees to be part of the solution, and the effort has drawn a tremendously positive response. Around the state of Georgia 14,000 employees have become a new resource for speakers at the PTA, the Rotary Club, and the Elks. They are a resource in every community to help raise money for prevention and other programs. The employees, including young people, appreciate receiving straight health information for their own good, the good of their company, and the safety of their colleagues. But they also appreciate the appeal not to let drug and alcohol problems happen to those around them—an appeal to decency. Many young workers particularly have said that no one ever asked them to help before; it was assumed that they were the problem.

Many companies that are mounting drug education programs for cost efficiency are keeping interesting figures on what is happening to absenteeism, utilization of health services, job and product safety, and liability charges for people who fall off the dam when they are stoned. This effort is imaginative, with new companies getting involved, and there will be much to learn from it.

ALFRED MCALISTER, University of Texas Health Sciences Center

Historically in the field of public health, huge political battles were fought before sanitary reform was accomplished. It was finally achieved when large industrialists realized that in order to concentrate a productive labor force in a city, people had to be provided with clean water. When industrialists saw that their profits would be maximized by a large-scale public health measure, they took action. There has been a revolutionary change in recent years as employers have taken responsibility not only for job-related diseases, a trend that has a long history, but for their workers' non-job-related diseases, seeing the relationship not only to productivity but also to their share of health care costs. Large corporations will have enormous power in health planning in the future.

MARILYN GOLDWATER, Maryland House of Delegates

Another group that needs to be a part of this picture is the insurance industry. Their reimbursement policies dictate what kinds of programs and services are available. Although they call it health insurance, the companies tend rather to provide illness insurance. I think that we need to explore with them the benefits to society and to the industry itself of changing their reimbursement policies somewhat to become education-oriented, not just treatment- or illness-oriented.

BEN MASON, Adolph Coors Company

Many of the beverage manufacturers have established wellness clinics for their employees, are very aggressively pursuing the participation of employees in educational and training sessions, and are working to develop cost-effectiveness data. These positive contributions to health promotion are an important commitment on the part of these firms, and I think that it is good to take note of it. We would be pleased to share what we are learning with the research and public health communities.

PATRICIA SCHNEIDER, Wine Institute

Wine Institute—whose president, John DeLuca, I represent—has great access to and communication with its members. We can talk to our members about advertising practices, moderation, and safe drinking concepts in a way that those outside do not and perhaps cannot. The education process ought to include the active participation of all segments of the alcohol beverage industry.

LAWRENCE WALLACK, University of California, Berkeley

What should be the relationship between the government role and the other roles we have talked about? I think that what matters is that a relationship exists. One of the ways the panel's report is different from past efforts is that it no longer sees alcohol-related problems as primarily individual problems, but starts to see them as systems problems. When we talk about systems problems, we identify things that exist on many different levels—individuals, schools, families, communities, social institutions. We cannot work on all of these levels all the time, but we can have as a goal the development of actions and purposes that are consistent across these levels. Too much comes out in the form, "It is this or that" and not enough in the form, "It is all of these things, and each has to be developed and constructed in relation to the development and construction of the others." A single program in and of itself may not make a detectable difference, but in relation to other strategies, both individual and aggregate, every individual effort may in fact serve a very important function.

5 Alcohol and the Mass Media

TELEVISION PROGRAMMING, ADVERTISING, AND THE PREVENTION OF ALCOHOL-RELATED PROBLEMS

LAWRENCE WALLACK, University of California, Berkeley

There is a tale, often told in public health circles, about a health worker walking alongside a river. Suddenly there is the sound of a person thrashing about in the water and a cry for help. The health worker leaps into the water and pulls out the drowning person. Just as the victim is being revived, there is another cry for help, and the same process is repeated. This happens several more times until it finally strikes the health worker that she or he is so busy pulling people out of the water that there is no time to explore upstream to determine how people are falling or being pushed into the river.

Our society has taken a primarily downstream approach to meeting human needs. We wait for people to develop problems and then invest substantial resources in an effort to rescue them. Once pulled out of the river, these people are then sent back into the same social system that was a significant part of the problem to begin with.

Prevention means shifting the emphasis of our efforts upstream to address the conditions that give rise to and sustain the problems that ultimately emerge downstream. We need to undertake long-term planning that addresses the many contributory causes to a problem and involves a difficult process of rethinking our basic assumptions about health. Such a shift is not practically or politically easy. Significant

79

economic and ideological interests are strongly vested in the existing system. Such interests are sure to question any redefinition of the problem or reexamination of basic assumptions that underlie how we view these problems (Beauchamp, 1976; McKinlay, 1979; Wallack, 1982; Ratcliffe and Wallack, 1983).

The purpose of this paper is to briefly examine the role that mass communication plays in the prevention of alcohol-related problems, focusing particularly on advertising and television programming. In doing so it attempts to move upstream and look at how mass media may be one of the environmental determinants of alcohol-related problems.

The upstream country can be described by identifying three specific territories. First, there is the regulatory system that serves to limit or enhance the availability of alcoholic beverages. It entails formal rules and laws that attempt to reduce the supply of alcohol in society. Examples are regulations determining who can buy alcohol, when and where it can be purchased, how much it costs, etc. A secondary emphasis of the system is to legislate a safer environment so that when drinking does take place the consequences may be less severe. Passive restraints in cars and safer consumer products are two examples of this approach.

A second territory contains informal rules that structure the immediate environment in which drinking takes place. The expectation is that the microenvironment of drinking can be made safer through voluntary approaches. The current emphasis on server intervention programs is an example of this approach. The two primary differences between this territory and the first one is that these strategies are voluntary, and there is a much greater emphasis on the influence of the environment on behavior.

The third territory is education regarding the effects of alcohol and the appropriate use of alcohol in society. This education has many sources, including peers, family, teachers, and mass media. Education about drinking and appropriate alcohol use is also conveyed by the messages reflected in the arrangement of the other two territories. For example, heavier concentrations of outlets that offer easy availability of alcoholic beverages reflect an attitude of the larger community regarding alcohol use. The way parties and other entertainment activities are structured can also provide strong messages about alcohol use.

The most common understanding of alcohol education is through the schools or planned mass media campaigns. This paper, however, addresses the unplanned types of alcohol education that occur during television programming and advertising.

The prevention of alcohol-related problems is an ambitious task. For such an undertaking to make progress toward a realistic goal, it must address the problem on each of the levels on which it exists—a major objective being consistency of purpose and action across the entire system. It makes little sense to educate schoolchildren about responsible drinking or decision making, or to educate communities through mass media campaigns that people should, if they drink, drink in moderation, when the larger physical and social environment is laden with messages that directly contradict the content of the educational approach. This is not to say that specific skills to facilitate safer drinking practices cannot be taught in the classroom or through mass media campaigns. The potential success of these efforts or their possible failure will, however, be greatly affected by the supportiveness of the rest of the environment in which social behavior and alcohol use takes place.

Television and Health Behavior

The television set is a fixture in virtually every American household. Recent estimates indicate that 98 percent, or almost 78 million, of the homes in the United States have at least one television set. On the average, Americans watched approximately 30 hours of television per week in 1981 (*World Almanac,* 1981). For children, television can be a major mechanism of socialization. By the time a boy or girl graduates from high school, he or she will have spent more time in front of a television set (17,000 hours) than in a formal classroom (11,000 hours). From early childhood through the high school years, television viewing consumes more time than any other single activity except sleeping (Rubinstein, 1978). The media are now being recognized as a major source of observational learning and a definer of cultural norms (Hamburg and Pierce, 1982). Nonetheless, educators in general and health educators in particular pay far too little attention to the media as a source of education.

Television is a source for a range of information but appears to be an especially important source of health information for a substantial number of adults. Gerbner and his colleagues (1981:904) suggest that television "may well be the single most common and persuasive source of health information." Unfortunately a great deal of this information is of questionable accuracy (Greenberg, 1981) and may contribute to the adoption of unhealthy behaviors in the viewing audience. A more conservative notion is that heavy exposure to such programming may decrease the likelihood of individuals adopting preventive behaviors (Gerbner et al., 1981) rather than cause the adoption of negative behaviors.

A causal connection between television viewing and health behavior has yet to be explored. Over the past 15 years, however, the number of studies on the effect of televised violence on children has grown considerably. Although there are still those who dispute the causal connection (e.g., Milavsky et al., 1982), the overwhelming sense of the scientific community supports the causal relationship. Given that the level of violence on television has not declined since the original surgeon general's program on television and violence (Signorielli et al., 1982), television may be seriously influencing the status of the society's health by continuing to portray high levels of violence.

Although there have been well over 2,000 studies of the effects of televised violence on children, virtually no attention has been paid to the effects of televised portrayals of alcohol use on viewers. When Comstock (1976) reviewed the scientific literature for the Hathaway hearings (U.S. Senate, 1976) on media images of alcohol, he could not find one scholarly reference on alcohol and mass media. What did exist was a series in the *Christian Science Monitor* (Dillin, 1975a,b,c) on alcohol use on prime-time programming and a book chapter that only briefly addressed portrayals of alcohol on television in the early 1970s (Winick and Winick, 1976). Since the hearings, several research studies analyzing the content of prime-time television portrayals of alcohol have been conducted (Greenberg et al., 1979; Breed and DeFoe, 1981; Greenberg, 1981; Gerbner et al., 1982). The findings of these studies are presented below.

Television Programming As Alcohol Education

There is increasing concern about the role television plays in the construction of reality. At the recent White House Conference on Families (1980:92), one participant noted:

Television has become another member of the family. We eat meals near it, we learn from it, we spend more time with it than any single individual. Television is central in our children's lives, as a tutor; babysitter; teacher; entertainer; and sales-person all rolled into one.

Delegates to this series of conferences rated the overglamorization of alcohol and drugs in television programming and advertising as a priority area for attention. The content analysis of alcohol portrayals on prime-time programming and the existing theoretical basis for the potential effects of such programming suggest that the concern of parents, consumer groups, and some scientists is justified. What kind of alcohol education is being offered by one of America's more prominent teachers?

The *Christian Science Monitor* series by John Dillin looked at prime-time (8-11 pm) shows in the spring of 1975. Scenes involving alcohol were found on 201 of the 249 shows studied—81 percent. (The definition of drinking must be considered very loose, i.e., it had only to be mentioned to be counted.) The most popular beverage, alcoholic or otherwise, was found to be distilled spirits. This is somewhat ironic because, as Dillin points out, the advertising of this product is prohibited through industry self-regulation (Dillin, 1975a).

In a later article, Dillin (1975b) reported on a brief study that the National Institute on Alcohol Abuse and Alcoholism (NIAAA) conducted as a background piece to meetings with network officials. The 2-day study looked at soap operas as well as prime-time programming and found levels of alcohol involvement as high as those reported in the *Christian Science Monitor* article. Although no details on the study were provided, Dillin reported the identification of four aspects of alcohol use on television: the frequent use of alcohol, the humorous portrayal of drunkenness, the use of alcohol as a problem solver, and the portrayal of alcohol use as glamorous, sophisticated, and mature. The latter three types of alcohol portrayal subsequently became key elements in NIAAA's public information campaigns, which tried to change attitudes about alcohol. This is again somewhat ironic, in that the emphasis on alcohol use, which is contrary to the National Association of Broadcasters (NAB) code, continued even while the media provided some public service time presumably to counter conditions to which the code violations contributed.

A final *Christian Science Monitor* article (Dillin, 1975c) reviewed prime-time programs in the fall of 1975. Despite NIAAA's efforts to work with writers and the networks, the study of 71 programs indicated little difference between the new season and the previous one. Keyed by the brief federal study that had been done in the interim, the *Christian Science Monitor* found gratuitous use of liquor, inappropriately humorous portrayals of drunkenness, the association of drinking with sophistication, and the use of alcohol as a tension reliever. Alcohol consumption, particularly the use of distilled spirits, was found to be far out of proportion to the use of other, more common beverages that people actually consume.

A brief study of drinking on soap operas was conducted before the *Christian Science Monitor* study but was not reported until late 1977. Garlington (1977) used four women observers to assess the rate of drinking on soap operas. A total of 79 half-hour segments were viewed over a 5-day period and were coded on the basis of actual drinking or reference to drinking and the setting in which drinking took place. Drinking was classified in three categories: verbal reference, drinking scene, and/or background drinking. The reason for drinking was also recorded but was not reported because of low observer reliability. The study found that there were 236 events involving alcoholic beverages, or three events per show. There were 205 soft drink events coded, for an average of slightly more than 2.5 per show. The use of distilled spirits was greater than wine or beer consumption, and the most common setting for consumption was the home.

Recently a reanalysis of Garlington's data (Calfiso et al., 1982:1241) found that drinking most often occurred in the home and was most commonly done as a relief from stress. The findings, according to the research team, suggest that alcohol use is generally not troublesome and is an integral part of normative behavior.

Breed and DeFoe (1981) reviewed prime-time television shows during the 1976-1977 season. The review included the top 15 situation comedies and the top 15 dramatic series taken from the Nielson ratings after 5 weeks of the new television season. The study covered 14 weeks and 150 hours of air time. Scenes that indicated significant alcohol use were noted and studied in detail. To be considered significant the scene had to meet one of seven criteria: portrayal of heavy drinking; a purpose in drinking that went beyond sociable sipping; a consequence that probably would not have occurred if a nonalcoholic beverage had been ingested; some response to drinking activity by another person; an evaluation of drinking as good or bad; a contribution of drinking behavior to the plot or characterization; or humor that reflected on any of the criteria listed above.

They reported that almost 60 percent of the drinking scenes observed involved heavy drinking (five or more drinks) or chronic drinking. Compared with the U.S. population this would be considered atypical drinking, since only about 25 percent drink as many as five drinks in a given situation (Clark and Midanik, 1981). Similar to results of past studies, distilled spirits were the beverage of choice, and the most frequent reason for consumption was in response to a crisis or as a social prop. Although drinking was common and heavier drinking was the mode, the researchers reported little disapproval of alcohol abuse, and when disapproval was seen it tended to be mild. In addition, more often than not no serious consequences of alcohol abuse were shown (Breed and DeFoe, 1981).

The study also compared televised portrayals of consumption of alcoholic beverages, soft drinks, coffee, and water with estimated actual consumption. They found that television consumption of alcoholic beverages was higher than for other beverages, despite the opposite relationship existing in the real world. For example, the consumption of alcoholic beverages was first on television but last in actual per capita consumption data among the four categories of beverages considered.

Nicholas Johnson, former commissioner of the Federal Communications Commission, had done a similar comparison in testimony at the Hathaway hearings (U.S. Senate, 1976); he compared beverage use not only to actual consumption but also to the level of advertising of the product. He found a direct relationship between frequency of advertising and how often a product is consumed and also found the televised use of alcoholic beverages to be greatly out of proportion to their actual use.

The researchers also coded the context of drinking and found—to some extent in contrast to the findings of Garlington (1977)—that although 58 percent of the drinking in situation comedies took place in the home, only 29 percent of the drinking in dramatic series was done in a domestic setting. One interesting point was that 25 percent of the drinking took place before or during work.

Overall, four purposes of drinking were identified. First, drinking was seen as a response to personal crises. Second, drinking was seen as secondary to other activities and used as a social lubricant or as something to do while standing around. (This is much the way that cigarettes were used in the mass media in the 1940s and 1950s.) The third and fourth purposes, ceremonial drinking and drinking for manipulation, were found with limited frequency.

A group of Michigan State researchers examined a composite week of network programming for the 1976-1977 and 1977-1978 seasons. The sample included one episode of each prime-time and Saturday morning fictional series. The researchers observed approximately 80 shows representing 60 hours for each season (Greenberg et al., 1979:4). Substance use was broadly defined as "that set of behaviors that included each incident of the consumption of, attempt to consume, inducement to consume, and making laudatory remarks about the consumption of alcohol."

In the 1976-1977 season alcohol use was observed 2.19 times per hour; the next season it had increased to 2.66 times per hour. This use was highest between 9 and 11 pm (4.92 times per hour in the 1977-1978 season) and on situation comedies and crime shows (over 4.5 times per hour in the 1977-1978 season).

The most recent study on television and drinking also comes from Michigan State University (Greenberg, 1981). The top 10 prime-time fictional series of 1980 and the top-rated soap operas were observed. Four episodes of each of the prime-time series were reviewed along with eight episodes from the soap operas. Greenberg (1981:12) reported that "television characters may not smoke or use drugs, but they drink with prodigious frequency." The rate of alcohol consumption far exceeded that reported in earlier seasons, averaging 8.13 incidents of alcohol consumption per hour on the 10 top-rated prime-time series. Soap opera drinking was substantially lower, at 2.25 events per hour, or slightly fewer than Garlington (1977) had found. Similar to the Breed and DeFoe (1981) study, alcohol use was shown in an almost entirely positive context, with no indication of potential risk.

The research of Gerbner and his colleagues (1982:298) on the Cultural Indicators Project at the Annenberg School of Communication has recently been summarized in the area of health. The data on alcohol, stretching back several years, indicated that over one-third of major television series characters drink, but only about 1 percent have a drinking problem. In general, drinking was found to be widespread and condoned.

It would appear that drinking on television has not changed much since the *Christian Science Monitor* series. It should be remembered, however, that we don't know what level of drinking would be shown were it not for the information provided by the studies that have been conducted. But what difference does it make that drinking is shown so frequently on television? It really makes little sense to compare consumption of water, soda, or alcoholic beverages on television with their actual consumption in real life. Television deals with smaller than 24-hour segments of people's lives. For example, if we compared the rate of drinking of characters on television with that of a real person coming home from work, the rate of drinking on television might more closely mirror real life. The frequency of drinking per se may tell us little. The larger implications of drinking on television, however, can be seen in two ways. First, is the drinking process shown accurately? That is, are the risks as well as the benefits of alcohol conveyed in a clear fashion? Second, what is the potential theoretical importance of frequent, non-problematic portrayals of drinking on television? Scholarly articles on television and drinking rely substantially on Bandura's (1977) social learning theory for discussing this topic. Bandura suggests that exposure to content stimuli that are consistent in theme and are seen with considerable frequency can affect the viewer. Greenberg and his colleagues (1979:10-11) note:

To the extent that social behaviors on television, such as acts of drinking, are performed by liked characters, in a positive context, without negative consequences, or with positive rewards, social learning is more likely to occur. Such learning can take several forms. It can affect the viewer's aspirations and expectations about the observed behaviors; it can impinge on the viewer's beliefs with regard to the acceptability or appropriateness of the behavior, it can teach the behavior, and it can induce either imitation or a desire for imitation. To the extent that the behavior is a common one, with the implements easily accessible, then the likelihood of such learning is further enhanced.

Another related theoretical issue is time frame. For example, a few drinking incidents per show may not seem like a great deal of exposure. When this exposure is stretched over a year, considering current levels of television viewing and alcohol-related incidents, a person under the legal drinking age will be exposed to more than 3,000 acts of drinking over the course of a year (Greenberg et al., 1979). This level of exposure, which does not include commercial messages about alcohol, is a continuing reinforcement of inaccurate health information. It is a major contributor to the shared symbolic environment in which we interact (Gerbner et al., 1982).

In summary, television has not been a very good educator about drinking in society. The rate of drinking on television is greater than that in real life and the rate of problems associated with drinking tends to be much lower. Despite the NAB's position that alcohol use should be deemphasized on television, this has clearly not been the case. Television in general has probably served to legitimize increased use of alcohol by conveying the image that it is acceptable or even required to drink in an expanding array of situations (Breed and DeFoe, 1981). If indeed alcohol is a major public health problem and, as the panel estimates, is responsible for 50,000-75,000 deaths annually—you could not find this out from watching television.

Advertising As Alcohol Education

While television programming may be inadvertently educating viewers about alcohol use, advertising uses sophisticated and highly specialized techniques to educate consumers about the uses and rewards of alcohol. As might be expected, advertising seeks to place the product in the best possible light and is little, if at all, concerned with its possible adverse consequences. Thus the "education" the consumer receives from advertising is severely limited. As Neubauer and Pratt (1981:217) note, the outcome of the advertising exchange is always in the interest of the producer and only rarely in the interests of the consumer:

Examination of the advertiser's message reveals that the objective of selling outweighs, to the point of defrauding, the objective of providing information. Consumers are left to make empty choices. They cannot know enough to make substantive distinctions between apparent options. We have the illusion of information and the reality of people making psuedo-choices. Those pseudo-choices often lead consumers to act against their own interests.

Well over $1 billion will be spent on alcoholic beverage advertising in 1984. We will hear it on radio and see it on billboards, television, magazines, buses, subways, calendars, sports schedules, and most any other place where space is available. In 1979 beer producers alone purchased $369 million worth of print and broadcasting space (*Bottom Line*, 1981). In 1980, alcoholic beverage advertisers spent $903 million on "measured" media—magazines, radio, television, newspapers, and outdoor placements (*Monday Morning Report*, 1981). This includes over $316 million in advertising space purchased for distilled spirits (*Liquor Handbook*, 1981) and $134 million worth of placements of wine advertising (*Wine Marketing Handbook*, 1981). Numerous other types of advertising, such as sponsorship of various athletic and cultural events and on-site, point-of-sale promotions, are not included in the advertising figures. These estimates also do not include the production costs for these creative and technically sophisticated advertisements. The attention of the American public is clearly the focus of intense competition among alcoholic beverage producers.

Advertising permeates every facet of our daily lives, and many of the messages run counter to good public health practices. Such messages often misleadingly link the attainment of valued ends to product use. It is somewhat ironic that advertising, often justified on the basis of providing useful information to the consumer in order to facilitate informed choice, is so often subtly false and misleading. Goldsen (1980), commenting on television commercials, notes that prices and terms are rarely specified, product descriptions are vague and ambiguous, and the names of the real corporate owners are seldom heard. Alcohol advertisers rely heavily on persuasive messages that have little or nothing to do with the product. In a content analysis of alcohol advertisements in national magazines, Breed and DeFoe (1979) found wealth, prestige, and success to be an "indirect promise" made in 28 percent of such ads. Social approval or acceptance as a consequence of product use was coded in 23 percent of the ads reviewed. In general the researchers found "little logical relationship between the product and the advertised message." Content relevant to public health concerns, such as cautions regarding the negative effects of excessive drinking, were "seldom mentioned."

Mosher and Wallack (1979b), commenting on proposed reforms in the advertising of alcoholic beverages (federal regulations have not been revised since their promulgation in the early 1930s), concluded that alcoholic beverage advertising is misleading in two ways: (1) Alcoholic beverages are promoted by appeals to desires and needs that are irrelevant to the product. (2) The absence of accurate health information in the marketing of a product with serious public health consequences hampers the consumer in making an informed choice.

A recent major study of the effects of alcoholic beverage advertising has produced findings that are cause for concern for those involved in promoting public health. A team of Michigan State University researchers found that advertising was a significant informal source of socialization about alcohol for adolescents and that there was "little doubt that alcohol advertising exerts an influence on the frequency and quantity of adult alcohol consumption" (Atkin and Block, 1980:18). As might be expected, these findings have generated some controversy; in fact the study, funded by four federal agencies, was released only after extensive delay. These findings contradict a larger body of previous research that has failed to indicate a relationship between advertising and increased alcohol consumption (most of this literature has been summarized in Pittman and Lambert, 1978).

Two recent studies on the content of alcoholic beverage advertising in national magazines (Strickland et al., 1982) and television (Finn and Strickland, 1982) indicate little concern over the content of the ads. Examination of 640 unique magazine ads found that the controversial themes identified by critics of alcoholic beverage advertising were infrequent. The most frequent themes were product-related and addressed information, quality, and traditions or heritage. Although the 131 unique television ads studied were more likely to use hazardous or exotic activities to promote products, these ads were also found to be generally free of controversial themes (Finn and Strickland, 1982).

There are several reasons for the conclusions of the Breed and DeFoe study to differ so greatly from those of Finn and Strickland, and Strickland et al. The differences are due to methodological as well as ideological issues. For example, the construction of the coding categories is essential to the content analysis method. The instructions to coders as to what is allowed in each category essentially determines the outcome of the study. The Strickland et al. (1982) and Finn and Strickland (1982) studies provided the following instructions to coders for the "sexual connotations" category: "Do not code this theme 'present' for such things as: -Good-looking or sexy models that are less than 'provocative' or -Models that are simply 'showing skin,' but are less than provocative" (Finn and Strickland, 1982:987). For the "wealth and affluence" category, coders were instructed: "Do not code this theme 'present' for such things as: -Average wealth portrayed on television (most ads show people who are well-off; this category is only for wealthy appeals)" (p. 983).

Yet in an important way the debate about the content and effects of alcoholic beverage advertising is interesting but somewhat irrelevant. The analysis of content and effects cannot be separated from the larger marketing mix of price, physical availability, and general institutional and social support for drinking. In addition, such analysis cannot be separated from researchers' disciplinary training and the values inherent in their backgrounds.

In summary, the debate over what alcoholic beverage ads are "really" saying and what effects such ads might have may never be resolved. The advertising issue is primarily one of public policy; science, in its traditional form, can contribute in only a limited way. As I have noted elsewhere (Wallack, 1981), the fundamental issue that we need to address is whether the wide-scale promotion of alcoholic beverages is consistent with the goals of a society concerned with minimizing the social, economic, and personal hardship associated with current levels of alcohol-related problems. Facts themselves play a smaller role in determining policy than how we determine which facts to choose and the values we hold to interpret these facts. Empirical studies analyzing the content of alcoholic beverage ads are based in part on personal value orientations. The numerous decisions that researchers must make as they frame their questions, construct their categories for the data, and elect what to analyze and what to ignore all involve subjective judgments.

At a time when many consumer groups are entering the debate over the wisdom of massive alcoholic beverage advertising, the research that is expedient will be used to hammer a particular viewpoint. This is an important part of the process of establishing reasonable public policy. It may well be that the traditional tools of science simply cannot provide the clarity in this area necessary to resolve major issues: the ensuing debate on advertising must also be a debate on the role of science in determining social policy.

Even without conclusive studies to show that advertising is a poor educator on alcohol, there can be little doubt that health education is not the primary point of such ads. In an interview with *Business Week,* Edgar Bronfman, chairman and chief executive of Seagram Co. Ltd., showed a different side than most industry leaders on the issue of advertising. Rather than touting informational value and arguing against the thesis that such advertising appeals to the consumer to drink excessively, Bronfman (*Business Week,* 1981:139) told the interviewer:

You can get just as drunk drinking cheap stuff as expensive stuff. So what you're really selling is glamour and an impression.

Another recent *Business Week* article focused on wine marketing trends. The entry of the Coca-Cola company into the wine market, much like the entry of the Philip Morris Company into the beer market, has led to a marketing explosion. Coca-Cola's goal, according to *Business Week* (1982:110), is to establish wine as a beverage that can be consumed at any time in any place:

[T]he industry's key to doubling wine sales is to get its product message across to potential customers. Wine advertising spending has already leaped from $55 million in 1970 to about $136 million last year (1981) and is likely to double again in 1985.

The expected effect of more aggressive wine marketing in general is illustrated in the comment of John Senkevich (quoted in *Council on Alcohol Policy Quarterly Newsletter,* 1983:7), president of Geyser Peak Winery:

By picking up on the merchandising, selling and distribution of the soft drink industry, the wine industry can change the image of wine to a regularly consumed beverage as opposed to today's image of a special occasion drink.

In reference to televised beer commercials, Richard Cohen (1983), writing in a syndicated Associated Press column, made the following comments:

Call them 30 second lies or a shuck or anything you want, but what you don't see in the commercials is what happens to the customers they are aimed at. It's understandable. For many of them, "Miller Time" leads to the hardest time of all.

Strategies for Change

The prevention of alcohol-related problems requires far-reaching strategies that address the conditions contributing to the development and maintenance of these problems. The mass media, particularly through television programming and advertising, are important contributors to the social environment in which drinking takes place. The message of the media is not consistent with the serious public health implications of alcohol use. Indeed, advertising and repeated portrayals of drinking on television may well contribute to alcohol-related problems. Although the causal relationships needed to satisfy most scientists and industry representatives will never be absolutely proven, this should not deter others from promoting specific actions to remedy the communication of misinformation on alcohol through advertising and television programming.

Television Programming   George Gerbner has said: "If you can write a nation's stories, you needn't worry about who makes its laws. Today television tells most of the stories to most of the people most of the time." Television is waking up to its role as an educator on alcohol. Recently the Caucus for Producers, Writers, and Directors sent out a "white paper" to its members. Ostensibly this action, reported 22 February 1983 in the newspapers, was actually a reaction to the crash, caused by a drunk driver, that seriously injured actresses Mary Martin and Janet Gaynor and killed Martin's manager.

The one-page paper, titled "We've Done Some Thinking," asked whether

. . . any of us as members of the creative community in Hollywood unwittingly glorified the casual use of alcohol in one of our projects? Have we written it as macho? Directed it as cute? Produced it as an accepted way of life? In short, are we subliminally putting a label of "perfectly okay" on alcohol related behavior and selling it to the American people? . . . The answer we fear is yes.

The paper went on to list seven remedial suggestions based on the work of Breed and DeFoe.

Warren Breed and James DeFoe (1982) developed a process called "cooperative consultation" to work with media personnel. This technique has been used successfully with the comic book and television industries. Cooperative consultation is based on the assumption that industries will be willing to correct a problem when it is tactfully and convincingly brought to their attention.

Cooperative consultation is a four-part process. First comes research. Breed and DeFoe conducted detailed content analysis of drinking on television over a period of several years, researched television production methods so they could frame their findings and suggestions in an acceptable way, and became well informed on issues related to alcohol problems and alcoholism. From research the process moves to general education of the industry (in this case all those involved in the many stages of television production). This included a series of presentations to the Standards and Practices Office of two of the three networks, extensive personal contacts with writers, and the development of a newsletter on alcohol topics that was widely distributed to industry people. The next stage is specific education. This stage was reached when someone requested further information, which often took the form of a request for help on specific problems on scripts addressing alcohol-related issues. To meet these requests DeFoe, a member of the Writers Guild, offered a series of alternatives that could move the script along but not at the cost of providing inaccurate information about alcohol. The final part of the process is feedback from the industry (Breed and DeFoe, 1982).

In a sense, the apparent success of Breed and DeFoe is in part due to the way that they have carefully developed their project as a resource for the industry. In this case both the industry and the viewer benefit. The process of research, general and specific education, and feedback fits well with a constructive, active approach to prevention. This process has been effective in attaining change in media portrayals of alcohol use, and several excellent examples of the outcome of this process are available (Breed and DeFoe, 1982).

The caucus's white paper also indicates the success of this approach. It is certainly premature to suggest that the cooperative consultation process has changed the way that alcohol is portrayed substantively enough to create larger change in the social environment of drinking. Nonetheless, the work of Breed and DeFoe and the response by the caucus are extremely positive indications that television will be a more knowledgeable and accurate source of information on alcohol than it has been in the past.

The content analysis work of Breed and DeFoe should be continued. An ongoing, annual analysis of alcohol portrayals on prime-time television is important for three reasons: first, as more consumer groups become involved in the debate over television, it will be important to have a solid data base to avoid distortions and exaggerations of how television is handling alcohol. At this time, this type of content analysis seems to generate little if any controversy, as does the same method applied to advertising. Second, the decision makers in the television industry are clearly interested in having this kind of data to guide their efforts. They *are* interested in not providing misleading information about alcohol use and appear quite willing to use the type of feedback that can be derived from these carefully collected data. Third, continued research in this area will allow us to monitor how well the media is responding to alcohol problems. At the same time, this research can keep us informed in general about this important issue.

Advertising   Although television may be inadvertently misinforming viewers about alcohol, advertisers are presenting "rigged demonstrations" (Goldsen, 1980) to make sure their "educational" point is not lost. If the task of education about health is to make health-generating choices less difficult and health-damaging choices more difficult (Milio, 1976), then advertising is a formidable barrier that must be overcome.

The Bureau of Alcohol, Tobacco, and Firearms (BATF) is the federal regulatory agent for alcoholic beverage advertising. It has been almost five years since BATF announced the pending revision of existing regulations and called for public comment. The bureau received more than 9,000 comments, over 99 percent of which favored significant curbs on alcoholic beverage advertising. Though there has been no final action to date, BATF's initial reaction was to ignore virtually all these comments and relax rather than tighten controls on advertising. Such advertising, for several reasons, is clearly misleading, yet the public's representative (BATF) has been and continues to be the handmaiden of the industry it should be regulating (Mosher and Wallack, 1979b, 1981; Wallack, in press), and it is unlikely that any change in this relationship will be forthcoming.

Continued research is needed on the content and effects of alcoholic beverage advertising. However, we cannot look for simple, concrete answers. Future work should emphasize the cumulative nature of advertising. Study of individual brand advertisements will tell us a little, but study of the broad nature of advertising and how it introduces, supports, and reinforces norms over time will greatly increase our understanding. As Dhalla (1978:87) notes: "Each piece of advertising influences sales today, and at the same time adds another brick to the structure of good will that increases business tomorrow." Advertising needs to be understood both historically and in relation to current broad systems of norms and values. Only by doing so can we understand the contradiction pointed out by an editorial in *Advertising Age* (quoted in *Bottom Line,* 1978): "A strange world it is, in which people spending millions on advertising must do their best to prove that advertising doesn't do very much!"

Future research must also acknowledge that advertising is purposeful. It tries to promote one end at the expense of some other. Advertising alone may not cause alcohol problems, but it certainly contributes to the development and maintenance of these problems in the community. The successes of advertising are therefore won at the expense of individuals and groups of people who suffer directly or indirectly from alcohol-related problems. Researchers must recognize the ethical implications involved in choosing which aspect of the effects of advertising to study. This subject does not permit value-neutral approaches; the very nature of the issue to be studied invokes conflicting values. Those who conduct research need to clarify the basic ethical assumptions on which their particular research strategy is based and to recognize the need for a balance of ethical perspectives.

There have been several excellent suggestions for strategies to deal with alcoholic beverage advertising. Consumer groups such as the Center for Science in the Public Interest (Jacobson et al., 1983) are injecting new enthusiasm into the advertising issue and building coalitions to press their perspective. The following suggested policies can serve as a starting point for further discussion.

• Withdraw the tax deduction for alcoholic beverage advertising. It has been estimated that 35 cents of every dollar of the more than $1 billion annually spent to place ads is deducted from corporate taxes (Mosher, 1983a). This amounts to over $350 million in lost tax revenue that is going to subsidize the misinformation campaigns of the alcoholic beverage industry.

• Levy a 10 percent tax on alcoholic beverage advertising to fund advertisements that show the other side of the alcoholic beverage story.

Conclusion

The prevention of alcohol-related problems should be a broad effort encompassing a range of strategies. The usual focus of prevention efforts since Prohibition has been the individual drinker, with little or no attention given to the producers, marketers, or distributors of alcoholic beverages. This has resulted in a narrow range of prevention strategies that usually rely on small-scale (school or community) efforts to alter attitudes and thereby change behavior, or a few large-scale mass media programs. Both types of programs, no matter how well planned or implemented, are unlikely to succeed because they exist in a generally hostile environment rich with messages supporting and encouraging the use and misuse of alcohol. The major contributor to this anti-education environment is clearly alcoholic beverage advertising. The massive amount of misleading information being disseminated through alcoholic beverage advertising acts as a barrier to the success of community-based programs and larger public information efforts. Television programming is also a great, though inadvertent, contributor to this vast reservoir of misinformation. Recent events, however, do suggest that major figures in the television industry are quite responsive to the seriousness of the public health problems generated by alcohol. A great deal more effort is needed in this area.

An effective prevention policy does not simply look at one small segment of the problem but seeks to comprehend the issues as they exist in a broader context. In my view, current policy seriously overemphasizes the responsibility of the individual drinker and underemphasizes the industry that produces alcohol and the government that regulates availability of the product. The role of the television industry has not been fully explored. A comprehensive policy should include attention to all these segments and ensure that a consistent, ethical responsibility to the consumer is carried out.

Even if we do accept the emphasis of current prevention strategies to persuade the individual to drink moderately, then it follows that the government must, at a minimum, ensure accurate consumer information. Currently this function is executed in two ways: First, the National Institute on Alcohol Abuse and Alcoholism (NIAAA), Division of Prevention and Research Dissemination, has funded a national public information campaign and provides current information at no charge through the National Clearinghouse for Alcohol Information. Second, the Bureau of Alcohol, Tobacco, and Firearms has the authority and the responsibility to regulate alcoholic beverage advertising. Even though these two agencies presumably serve the interest of the same public, their orientations are almost totally opposed.

In a recent year NIAAA allocated roughly $11.4 million to provide accurate alcohol information to the public (S. Maloney, personal communication, 1981). If we make an extremely liberal assumption and further estimate that each state spends approximately $1 million on prevention-related activities for the same purpose, the total still amounts to only half the 1978 advertising budget of the Anheuser Busch or the Miller Brewing companies, a pittance compared with the more than 1 billion tax-deductible dollars spent on alcoholic beverage advertising this year. This differential in spending is particularly disturbing because much alcohol advertising functions as an antieducation force. As Katzper and his colleagues (1978) have pointed out, the alcoholic beverage industry is quite willing to educate the public about the good life associated with alcohol but not about the potential negative consequences.

If we are serious about preventing alcohol-related problems, we need to start addressing some of the critical ethical issues that are evident in television programming and alcoholic beverage advertising. Yet work in this area alone will not make much of a dent in this significant public health problem. Only extensive action, planned and coordinated across the many levels on which the problem exists, will provide any hope for change.

DRINKING IN PRIME TIME: SHOW BUSINESS RESPONSIBILITY

LARRY STEWART, Caucus of Producers, Writers, and Directors

I am chairman of the Alcohol and Drug Abuse Committee of the Caucus of Producers, Writers, and Directors. The caucus is not a guild, a union, or a lobbying group; it is 160 individuals, many of whom are entrepreneurs involved in creating what the American public views on television every night. We formed this caucus to assume a more direct responsibility to the American viewing public in television programming and related fields: We wish to exercise our creative freedom in making television shows but we also know that what we do in our work has an impact on 70 million people every night.

In the autumn of 1982 three tragedies rocked Hollywood. First, Mary Martin and Janet Gaynor were critically injured in San Francisco when their taxi was hit by a drunk driver. Second, Natalie Wood, after a few glasses of wine, slipped off the side of a boat and drowned trying to do something she had done many times. And third, Bill Holden died alone in his room because he was too drunk to know he was bleeding to death. These tragedies helped wake us up and made us pay more attention.

Soon after Thanksgiving, CBS aired a local television series of five news pieces called "The Hollywood Alcoholic." The commentator, Carl Fleming, introduced George Peppard, Jan Clayton, Gary Crosby, Sheckie Green, and others—all familiar personalities who are admitted recovering alcoholics. As they talked about their own problems dealing with alcohol in their milieu and in films, a theme recurred: they were required from time to time, but more and more often, to perform with a drink in their hands. They began to think: "We are doing it too much. Every time we walk into a room, the ice is already there. We even walk into an elevator and someone says, 'Do you want a drink?' " They concluded that they had bought their own message and ended up alcoholics.

I watched that show, as did other people on our committee. We then got together to consider whether we, the creative artists who manufacture television, are putting a subliminal stamp on alcohol-related behavior as being perfectly all right. We discussed this in committee and decided, "We have found the enemy, and he is us." We went to the caucus as a whole and laid out to them the notion that maybe we portray alcohol use too much, that too much boozing happens on television. We know that we produce role models in this society, in the electric culture that we all live with. We looked around the room, at 160 people, and said: "Maybe we are all involved in this conspiracy."

The caucus charged our committee to find a way to reverse this trend. We relied heavily on the Breed and DeFoe studies, which were recommended by a director of "The Jeffersons" television show. The black community had come to "The Jeffersons" and said, "George Jefferson is giving us a bad role model for our kids." Breed and DeFoe worked on improving George Jefferson's image by limiting alcohol use on the show. Breed and DeFoe had also worked successfully with "M.A.S.H.," "All in the Family," "The Ropers," and "One Day at a Time." After carefully studying their research, we adopted their approach to the portrayal of alcohol use and abuse.

In carrying out our charge, we decided not to act like a pressure group; our business faces every pressure group that was ever born and we did not want to become colleagues pressuring each other. Our tactics were not to police, not to intimidate, but to create something that would make some sense to our colleagues. From this process came a white paper with the following suggestions.

1. Try not to glamorize the drinking or serving of alcohol as a sophisticated or an adult pursuit.

2. Avoid showing the use of alcohol gratuitously in those cases in which another beverage might be easily and fittingly substituted.

3. Try not to show drinking alcohol as an activity that is so "normal" that everyone must indulge. Allow characters a chance to refuse an alcoholic drink by including nonalcoholic alternatives.

4. Try not to show excessive drinking without consequences or with only pleasant consequences.

5. Demonstrate that there are no miraculous recoveries from alcoholism; normally it is a most difficult task.

6. Don't associate drinking alcohol with macho pursuits in such a way that heavy drinking is a requirement for proving one's self as a man.

7. Portray the reaction of others to heavy alcohol drinking, especially when it may be a criticism.

This white paper was sent to 4,000 writers, 2,300 directors, 700 producers, and all network heads. It also appeared in *Emmy* magazine, which has a subscription of 10,000 industry members. What it said is that we are all guilty of not paying enough attention to something. We used only one statistic: 26,000 alcohol-related traffic deaths each year. We asked our colleagues to join us in thinking about this problem and to see if there was a way to do a little less of what we have done so well—and yet so badly. And they seem to have joined us, the colleagues who are now saying, "My God, we never thought we were doing that. We didn't realize that Tom Selleck was drinking too much on 'Magnum.' " All of these role models, the Lou Grants, etc., always have a glass in their hands, and we sell this to the American public every night.

Our committee has attempted to bring an idea to the attention of the creative community and we feel confident that the community will respond on its own in a positive way. We think we are sensible and that our colleagues are going to react sensibly. We are not a policing or censorship body; we are not going to single out shows that violate our guidelines. We are not telling "Love Boat" that they should not have a bar; we are not telling "Cheers" or "Archie Bunker" to close down their sets because they take place in bars. But if drinking is not germane to the story, why show it? If it is germane, portray it, but do so with the awareness that the people we create become role models. That is what we are asking for: the awareness of our colleagues, a dedicated group that understands our impact in prime-time television and wants to be responsible about it.

ADVERTISING ALCOHOL: A RESPECTABLE, BILLION-DOLLAR-A-YEAR BUSINESS

STANLEY COHEN, *Advertising Age*

It is said that advertising is supposed to give information to the consumer. I think that is a hazardous formulation because the word "information" has a very special meaning to the people who use it. Advertising people give consumers the information that advertising people want them to have. The function of advertising is to serve the purpose of the advertiser. The advertiser pays for it, the advertiser takes the risk, the advertiser takes the penalty if it does not work. Advertising is not a public service when it is used to sell products. Any proposal that starts with the assumption that the advertiser owes something to the public in the advertising is built on sand.

For some people alcoholic beverage advertising is a moral and scientific issue. For some advertising people, however, it is a living—a profitable one. It is a challenge to their professional skills, a perfectly natural activity for experienced, upwardly mobile marketing and merchandising specialists who pursue the accoutrements of material success in a culture that tends to regard material success as a mark of excellence.

Any strategy to contain the perceived evils in the advertising and marketing of alcoholic beverages must take into account a number of fundamental political realities. I offer these questions and observations as a basis for discussion:

1. *How receptive are the industry and the public to the proposition that the advertising of alcoholic beverages should be subject to special restraints?* Historically, both the industry and the public believed that alcoholic beverage advertising was in fact a special case. When Prohibition ended, the marketing of beer, wine, and hard liquor resumed under the strongest regulatory schemes ever applied to mass-marketed products. The industry as well as the public was determined to prevent the return of the promotional abuses that had helped bring on Prohibition in the first place. During the 1940s and 1950s every alcoholic beverage ad was subject to prepublication clearance by federal regula-

tors. Federal rules and industry codes were devised to keep out anything resembling glamour. Liquor could not be associated with women, national heroes, patrotism, health, etc. Promotion was banned. Nothing but labels and institutional brand identification ads were permitted. Wine and liquor could not be advertised on the air.

But attitudes changed, and case by case, the rules changed as well. Someone got permission to use a picture of Mount Vernon in an ad; someone else showed a group enjoying drinks on the porch. The government decided it was pointless to preclear ads for an industry that was thoroughly familiar with the ground rules and had a fine record for staying well within the permissible areas. What seemed intolerable to a generation determined to prevent the return of the practices that had led to Prohibition had little meaning for a new generation more concerned about bureaucracy, restraints on free speech, and the inherent right to advertise products that are legally sold.

There is still little or no hard liquor advertising on the air. But Anheuser Busch and Heublein are among the top 25 television advertisers, and four brewers—Anheuser Busch, Schlitz, Coors, and Van Munching—are among the top 25 advertisers on radio. Moreover, there is no law barring hard liquor advertising from the air. A few outliers have already tested acceptance on offbeat radio stations. The code of the National Association of Broadcasters, which barred this type of advertising, recently folded up following an ill-advised antitrust attack from the U.S. Department of Justice. Given the permissive environment that has developed on so many other matters, I assume it is only a matter of time before liquor will be on television, too.

2. *What is the momentum behind liquor advertising?* Obviously money—but hardly Mafia money. The original distillers after Prohibition may have been ex-bootleggers and the beer industry may have been a mom and pop venture with hundreds of local and regional brands, but beer today is big money. Three giants, including Philip Morris, dominate that industry. (And now Coca-Cola has revolutionized the marketing of wine. As Kraft Foods discovered when it proposed to go into wine marketing, Wall Street analysts have a greater influence over who succeeds than the federal government does.) When you talk about restricting beer advertising, you talk about curtailing the money available for sponsoring professional football broadcasts on television, taking bread and butter from the mouths of 7-foot-tall basketball stars and superstar extra-point kickers.

In recent years the marketing of wine and beer in particular has gone through a significant transformation, which has made these beverages indistinguishable from other mass-marketed products. The entry of Philip Morris into the beer industry brought the fast-moving tactics of package goods marketing to beer: new brands and varieties, slickly researched and produced television campaigns, and well-organized marketing and sales promotion at the retail level. Under Philip Morris, Miller shook the industry by introducing Miller Lite. The number of major brewers is declining, but the variety of brands and packages proliferates. Every new brand and variety becomes a theme for more advertising—something to fill the time between innings in the ball games and during the time-outs at other sports events. Then of course there are the special promotions: the tennis tournaments, the race cars with Schlitz emblems, etc.

Essentially the same process took place in the wine industry. Coca-Cola acquired the Taylor brand in New York State and used it for a new series of wines produced in California. Actually, it farmed out production to Franzia Brothers and focused all its capital on marketing. By 1980, Coca-Cola was spending $30 million to advertise its Taylor brands, more than half as much as the entire industry had spent for advertising before its arrival. Two years after Coca-Cola became a figure in the wine industry, total wine industry ad spending nearly doubled. Industry experts estimate that on an investment of $150 million, Coca-Cola created a business worth $400 million.

3. *How good is your case?* Alcoholism is no doubt a sickness. Alcohol involves very serious health and safety issues. Is that enough in today's political and legal environment to win the kind of support needed to bring the power of the state into play? You have to assume that the other side is going to mobilize its own experts to fuzzy up the issues. It is a fact, for example, that some doctors do suggest that some of their older patients imbibe a bit as a tension reliever at the end of the workday. Skilled public relations people can get a lot of mileage out of that because it conforms to the daily experience of millions of people. It also fits neatly into a lobbying campaign based on the idea that how much alcohol to drink is something people ought to be free to decide for themselves.

Then, of course, there is the inevitable high-level scientific confrontation. There are experts expressing the view that evidence establishing a relationship between advertising and drinking is inconclusive. Before shrugging this off, I suggest you check with Peggy Charron of Action for Children's Television. It seemed obvious to her that a civilized society would be concerned about television ads that sell highly sugared breakfast cereals to young children. But by the time the public relations folks had done their thing, *The Washington Post* was denouncing the Federal Trade Commission (FTC) as a "National Nanny," pointing out that parents should decide what ads their children watch on television. In the end Congress rose up in righteous indignation, ordering the FTC to cease and desist from interfering with the constitutional right of children to know about breakfast cereals.

4. *And finally, what about the legalities?* True, there is something of a no-man's-land for liquor created by the states' rights provisions of the Twenty-first Amendment. But essentially the courts today take a dim view of any government effort to interfere with the dissemination of truthful information in advertising. When the government tried to stop Coca-Cola from running Taylor wine ads involving comparative taste tests on television, Coca-Cola won in court. Later, when the government tried to bar a claim that Chablis "light" wine has 25 percent fewer calories, the government lost again: It might be "unfair" to use some promotional themes in liquor ads or to fail to disclose hazards, but would the courts say it is "deceptive"? And in particular, would they say it is "deceptive" given the much more stringent definitions of "unfair" and "deceptive" that the Federal Trade Commission is recommending to Congress as part of the watered-down FTC act now moving through the legislative machinery?

Alcoholic beverages have achieved respectability and are marketed by the same people and through the same channels as soap, Chevys, and cigarettes. Inhibitions that existed after repeal of Prohibition have eroded, and the advertising and marketing strategies followed no longer distinguish alcoholic beverages from other products.

At the same time the scientific and legal issues have been effectively fudged by competent public relations and lobbying experts. The public's awareness of regulatory overkill in other product categories has helped neutralize the shock effect when health and safety issues arise, and our government—all three branches—is now controlled by officeholders who tend to worry more about property rights than consumer welfare.

That is the down side. There is another side: powerful religious and scientific support for restraint, and a residual recognition in the industry that the public has misgivings and that the industry would not necessarily prevail if its promotional activity were effectively challenged.

Many times in the past, efforts to test television advertisements for liquor were stopped merely because some powerful senator let it be known that this would not be acceptable. Congress does in fact have power to prohibit liquor advertising on the air if it opts to insert such restrictions in the licenses issued to broadcasters.

Drunk driving is something the public understands. Even the people now in power recognize that this counts more with the public than the property rights of alcoholic beverage advertisers.

In my presentation I have deliberately gone beyond the mere advertising of alcoholic beverages—although that in itself is a formidable activity, amounting to about $1 billion a year. A successful campaign to curb abuses in alcoholic beverage advertising begins with an honest evaluation of the nature of the economic and political clout behind this advertising. It requires a cohesive and realistic strategy. The odds are not attractive, but they are not impossible.

COMMENTS ON ALCOHOL AND THE MASS MEDIA

SHEILA BLUME, National Council on Alcoholism

The portrayal and interpretation of events and circumstances in our lives by the media extends beyond fictional characterizations in programming and advertising. Consider the deaths of four brilliant and talented men who died due to alcoholism, and the way their deaths were interpreted.

W.C. Fields died on Christmas Day, 1946, in a nursing home in Pasadena, California, with advanced cirrhosis of the liver. He bled to death from his gastrointestinal tract. His obituary in *The New York Times* said nothing about the cause of his death even though he made his living portraying an alcoholic, namely himself. Eight years later, in 1954, Dylan Thomas died after drinking 18 straight shots of whiskey in a hotel room in New York. *The New York Times* said only: "Dylan Thomas, noted Welsh poet, died yesterday in St. Vincent's Hospital of a cerebral ailment. He had been here on a lecture tour. His age was 39. Mr. Thomas collapsed last Wednesday night in his room at the Chelsea Hotel."

Contrast those earlier obituaries with that of Tennessee Williams, who died in 1983 at the age of 71; he choked to death on a bottle cap, which is a terrible way to die. The obituaries openly discussed the role of alcohol and drug abuse in his life, how it interfered with his creativity and caused great problems for him.

Finally, the *Phillips Exeter Academy Alumni Bulletin* recently reported the death of a member of the class of 1951: "He died of cirrhosis last December in New York City. Probably the outstanding member of our class, he earned a distinguished record at Yale, followed by an accelerated rise within the New York financial community, and a promising marriage. During his last years, his family life, his business career, and his life succumbed to alcoholism. His illness was refractory to attempts by many concerned friends, associates, and medical personnel to arrest the morose side of a unique and wonderful individual. He leaves two children, Andrew, 14, and Abigail, 10."

I think we should appreciate the sensitivity and honesty of that recent obituary even as we mourn the tragedy of the deaths of these talented, useful, brilliant, valuable people. We should hold this honesty in our minds as a standard when we look at communications about alcohol.

EDWARD BRECHER, West Cornwall, Connecticut

The mass media have clearly played a central role in molding popular views on alcoholism. Almost everyone knows, for example, thanks mainly to the mass media, that alcoholism is a disease and should be treated as a disease and that alcoholics cannot take just one drink. Since the media are so effective in establishing broad and simple generalizations in the popular mind, those of us concerned with alcohol education should be alert to other simple truths about alcohol that are ripe for dissemination today.

One is the very simple notion that alcohol is a drug, a mind-affecting, addicting drug. Far too many people continue to think of alcohol in one way and of marijuana, cocaine, LSD, and heroin in quite different ways. Sound public policies concerning alcohol as well as the other mind-affecting drugs are much more likely to emerge once the similarities are appreciated. The mass media are admirably suited to distribute this simple message—that alcohol is a drug—convincingly. However, there is a complication: Relatively few people understand what is meant when a drug is classified as addicting.

Let us tell them:

First, addicting drugs such as alcohol and heroin produce a phenomenon called tolerance. If someone drinks more than a threshold dose of alcohol week after week, it will take larger doses to produce a given level of excitement or sedation or disinhibition or inebriation next week than it took last week.

Second, addicting drugs such as alcohol and heroin produce a phenomenon called dependence. This means that a person who drinks a sufficient quantity of alcohol repeatedly will suffer withdrawal symptoms when the drinking is discontinued. If the doses are large enough and are taken over a long enough period of time, withdrawal symptoms may take the devastating form of delirium tremens (DTs). But the familiar alcohol hangover is in fact a milder withdrawal syndrome.

The third and fourth characteristics of an addicting drug are the most important and least publicized. Following withdrawal symptoms come a craving for the drug and a phenomenon known as drug-seeking behavior. Rats engage in drug-seeking behavior following withdrawal of either alcohol or heroin—and so do human alcoholics and heroin addicts.

These four phenomena—tolerance and dependence while drinking, craving and drug-seeking behavior following withdrawal—are what is meant when a drug is labeled as addicting. In developing future programs of alcohol education for the mass media accordingly, I urge that these ideas be high on the list of priorities.

MARK KELLER, Rutgers University

I am pleased that Mr. Brecher pointed out that *hangover* is a weasel word for withdrawal. He mentioned another weasel word, and that is *dependence*. Twenty years ago, the World Health Organization's expert panel tried to eliminate the word *addiction* from the expert lexicon in favor of the euphemism *dependence* for no other reason than that some members felt that *addiction* was a very severe word.

MARK MOORE, Harvard University

The debate over these terms seems to involve where the responsibility lies for bad drinking practices. If we say "addiction," it sounds like the drug or commodity is liable; if we say "dependence," it sounds like the responsibility is shared between the commodity and the user. The panel's report took the view that the effects came partly from the commodity and partly from the particular ways—at what rates, over what periods of time, and under what circumstances—people used it. That seemed to us a more accurate characterization, in many respects, than simply to say it is the drug.

EDWARD BRECHER, West Cornwall, Connecticut

It is the drug. Your report calls attention to a marvelous public health/anti–heart-disease campaign in California, which successfully reduced the consumption of eggs in one community by 66.6 percent. I defy anyone to develop an educational campaign that will reduce the consumption of alcohol by 66.6 percent.

BARRY SWEEDLER, National Transportation Safety Board

I think some of the most effective means of controlling smoking were the required smoking-and-health ads that were on television when cigarettes were advertised on television. When the smoking ads were dropped, the antismoking ads were dropped. Would it be appropriate to require antidrinking ads, to counteract some of the beer commercials? The beer industry spends $400 million annually on advertising. What if that same industry were required to set aside money for ads giving basic information on drinking and health?

HENRY KING, United States Brewers Association

There has been much conjecture regarding the purported impact of alcohol beverage advertising as it relates to the misuse of the product. However, in no way can this legitimate concern be construed as empirical research on the issue. Several years ago, the United States Brewers Association commissioned a major investigation of the role of alcohol beverage advertising in the use and misuse of the product (Finn and Strickland, 1982; Strickland, 1982a, 1982b; Strickland et al., 1982). Principally the findings emanating from this work demonstrated that beer advertising does *not* contribute to the abuse of the product. These scientific studies illustrate that there is no causal connection between the advertising of beer and the misuse of alcohol beverages.

LAWRENCE WALLACK, University of California, Berkeley

I discussed the Strickland et al. studies in my paper and the reasons why they diverge from the results of other studies. But I think there is a more fundamental issue here: Who controls the messages that are transmitted about alcohol? Who has access to the media? Where does the other side of the alcohol story get told? I am not talking about begging and scrimping to air an occasional public service announcement, or a campaign that appears once a year and is gone the other 364 days or 51 weeks of the year. What about the fact that alcoholic beverage advertising on prime-time television is a major source of misinformation about alcohol in society, which makes very difficult the task of all other alcohol educators—to communicate a consistent, accurate message about the use of alcohol?

PATRICIA SCHNEIDER, Wine Institute

California vintners are especially concerned about social messages conveyed in advertising, as exemplified in our advertising code. This session has focused almost exclusively on alcohol-related problems, advertising as "antihealth" education, and subliminal appeals to consumers that have little to do with the product. The California wine industry takes great exception to the failure to distinguish between beer, wine, and spirits, and the homogenizing effect of talking about wine as ethanol, a drug. When you talk about people's perceptions versus reality, a perspective on the cultural background and agricultural nature of wine is important.

I would like to express the philosophy of the California winegrowers and our educational materials. Wine Institute is a trade association of California vintners, representing approximately 95 percent of the California wine industry. We do not represent either wineries outside the state or makers of imported wines. We include several large firms, but the vast majority are small family operations. We are pleased that our 460 members all voluntarily subscribe to our Code of Advertising Standards. Those standards have been strengthened significantly over the past five years, and no violation of either the spirit or the letter of the code has occurred. We have a very specific educational approach in presenting California wine. Four aspects are emphasized consistently: promote the product responsibly; educate consumers about wine's proper use; emphasize the heritage of wine as a moderate mealtime beverage; participate in credible, innovative projects to reduce alcohol misuse.

Why have we taken these steps? Although the vast majority of our consumers use wine in moderation, we recognize that wine contains alcohol and can be misused; therefore, we have a responsibility as an industry, as concerned corporate citizens, to be part of the solution to the problem.

Highlights from the code: We hold overindulgence and intoxication to be absolutely unacceptable. We advocate integrated social contexts, in which wine is accompanied by food as a table beverage and drinking is not the focus of the activity. We prohibit the use of amateur or professional athletes, celebrities, and past or present heroes attractive to young people. We prohibit any suggestion of drinking and driving. And we discourage any association of wine with rites of passage. The code goes into greater detail about these specific provisions.

This code was not developed by an advertising firm or an outside or in-house public relations firm. It was developed over a year and a half, with groups of people sitting down in a room much like this, representing the alcoholism field, the media, public health, government representatives, and of course our own members, to get meaningful input about social issues raised and how we could best respond. Those organizations included the National Council on Alcoholism, the Alcohol and Drug Problems Association, the Health Education Foundation, the Association of Labor-Management Administrators and Consultants on Alcoholism, and the NIAAA, which was very helpful in those early stages, as were our sister industries, the brewers and the distillers. My remarks pertain only to the wine industry's advertising practices, but we feel that through this code, advertising plays an important role as a way to educate and teach consumers about the proper use of wine. That is a very important role in meeting both business and public health needs.

CHARLES CRAWFORD, Gallo Winery

Wine Institute has officially requested the U.S. Treasury Department to make this code of advertising standards mandatory, not only for wine, but also for beer and liquor. I do not know how far we will get, but we have asked for it to become an official part of the regulations.

MARK MOORE, Harvard University

As I read through this code of advertising standards and heard this presentation, I imagined the set of advertisements I see on television, and it seemed perfectly consistent. Would advertising that fit these guidelines be described by Breed and DeFoe and others who do content analysis as glamorizing alcohol?

PATRICIA SCHNEIDER, Wine Institute

From the research we have seen, no wine ads from our member wineries have fallen into the "glamorizing" category.

MARK MOORE, Harvard University

Every child wants to become a mature, successful adult. So in some sense the very image of responsible drinking might turn out to be inherently glamorous. I wonder whether the problem may be in the receiver, the child looking at the ads and trying to make a distinction between "me now" versus "what I aspire to be." The problem may be in wanting to aspire to that status too early.

JOHN DOYLE, National Council on Alcoholism

In Lincoln, Nebraska, junior high students are shown how seductive advertising can lead to false inferences such as "If your life-style involves drinking, then all these different things are going to happen." It may be illogical to reach these conclusions, but the advertising has become very sophisticated, so that you can jump to wrong conclusions, such as that you are going to be a macho person and succeed in all kinds of ways if you live the good life with this beautiful sparkling beverage. Kids quickly catch on; they go home and tell their parents, "We are being taken advantage of, we are being ripped off." I have no statistics because the program has not proceeded very far, but the preliminary results on student acceptance are amazing.

LAWRENCE WALLACK, University of California, Berkeley

There is certainly an interaction between factors inherent in the individual and different levels of reinforcement in the marketing systems and the larger social structure. When you look at just one ad—as some people have tried to ask, "Does this rock song about marijuana make people smoke marijuana?"—the answer is: Of course not. You have to take a much broader perspective.

STANLEY COHEN, *Advertising Age*

In the course of some 40 years in Washington I think I have heard every cause in the country argue that the solution to their problem is a big information campaign. When you deal with big institutional problems, you cannot conceive of the resources required for an effective information campaign. One notice, one poster, one public service announcement does not mean a thing. These solutions are not mutually exclusive, but a public information campaign is a slim reed—it has to be part of something else. It has to be part of a large, well-organized effort.

GEORGE HACKER, Center for Science in the Public Interest

Some people have used the metaphor of swimming against the tide and building a dam to stop the flow. The tide that I see is: Alcohol is easily available to young kids, many of them below the drinking age, at prices that make alcohol less expensive than soft drinks. We have promotions on college campuses and in the media encouraging drinking and portraying it as a sexy, great, adult, social thing to do (Jacobson et al., 1983). That tide affects all of us in one way or another. We need athletes and celebrities to get on the air as positive role models to say, "I drink occasionally, maybe one or two, but you will not find me out there drinking all night with the boys." But with a billion dollars of alcohol advertising out there, we obviously have to do a lot of positive portrayal to be effective.

6 Alcohol, Youth, Drunk Driving

WHAT PARENTS CAN DO

KEITH SCHUCHARD, Parental Resource Institute for Drug Education

Recognizing the Problem: An Intoxicating Media Environment

I am an English professor and I would much rather be teaching Milton and Spenser to adolescents than drug and alcohol information. But my own teenagers told me that all parents need "reality education" about popular culture and the everyday world in which kids are growing up. Otherwise, parents will be unable to communicate with their children, for we are out-communicated by a tremendous commercial industry—not just the advertising on television, but also T-shirts, comic books, and perfumes—a blitz of advertising without precedent. We are dealing with the widespread availability and commercial glamorization of plea-sure-giving chemicals. We are just now emerging from a decade in our history in which pleasure was deemed an extreme good, and adults taught that philosophy of hedonism to children and teenagers. This philosophy was accepted and encouraged by a large portion of the popular media and by advertising. Thus, we are dealing with an issue that we are hesitant to confront: chemicals that people like, that feel good, that are fun: alcohol, cocaine, marijuana, and whatever.

"Head shops" were a godsend to efforts in prevention, for they were a visible dragon: adults selling "space guns" to 8-year-olds to smoke marijuana in, doll-sized cocaine kits. Even naive parents could say, "Now, wait a minute, that seems a little bit out of line." Many lawyers and civil libertarian organizations went to bat for the head shops because they believed in a constitutional right to sell toy cocaine kits to kids. Fortunately, parents won most of those legal battles.

We are now facing something much more difficult, because the acceptability of selling intoxication has become so widespread. A generation of people are in positions of influence in the media, merchandising, and advertising worlds, a generation that came through the 1960s and linked up drug use with ideas of civil rights, liberation, and progress. In the old days, being liberal did not necessarily mean that you wanted your kids to smoke pot. But today the 34-year-old professional in the media industry who still uses drugs—and still links that use with connotations of fun, progress, intellectual enlightenment, etc.—is a big problem for network executives and filmmakers. Unfortunately, many merchandisers have worked aggressively, in a very predatory way, to lower the age of consumption of alcohol, drugs, and many other kinds of products. The industry talks about responsible marketing, but I see alcoholic milk shakes in stores and I hear advertising on teen-oriented radio stations for beer, wine, and other kinds of drinks.

Most parents and many health professionals do not know what life is like for an ordinary American kid. They should see what children see in the local shopping center—in the record stores, where songs glamorize alcohol and cocaine; in the T-shirt shops, where there is a tremendous increase in displays of drunkenness-oriented T-shirts. Here are some examples from the nicest gift shops and boutiques, in kiddie sizes for 6-year-old children: "Party till you puke." "Avoid hangovers, stay drunk." "Thank you for pot smoking—the American Cannabis Society." Here are some T-shirt messages for older children: "A day without dope is like a day without sunshine." "I don't have a drinking problem—I drink, I get drunk, I fall down. No problem."

Pro-drug advertising appears in the newspapers. Consider these movie ads in the *Atlanta Constitution,* a family newspaper: Richard Pryor, with his foot on fire from free-basing cocaine, is "America's funniest man." "Arthur"—99¢ at the kiddie special show—is drunk all the time and always very amusing and attractive. The movie "Personal Best" shows how to be a teenage Olympic aspirant: use Quaaludes and marijuana, smoke opium, drink tons of beer, and become a great athlete. Here are Cheech and Chong in "Still Smoking": the ad says, "You can smell the fun in the air. It has everybody rolling in the seats" (i.e., rolling marijuana joints). Drugs are even advertised on television. Cheech and Chong, the "lovable, furry comedians," are advertised during the morning cartoon hours smoking big joints. Rasta Man, on "Fridays," shows how to roll a giant marijuana cigarette while the audience chants along. "Saturday Night Live" has reruns at six o'clock in the evening with skits like "What this country needs is to put the cocaine back in Coca-Cola."

Drug-oriented comic books show kids how to shoplift and do drugs in the kitchen. The ad that appears first (probably the most expensive slot) in the April 1982 issue of *Seventeen* magazine is for Visine; it targets the teenage drinker and pot smoker: a boy who looks about 15 holds a drink up in his hand and points slyly to his eyes. The ad says: "When should you take the Visine test? After partying." Any sixth grader can tell you that means to get the red out of your eyes after you smoke pot, so your parents will not catch you. The magazine is read mainly by girls ages 10-14.

Hashish frisbees and marijuana dashboard pipes are found in many of America's nicest gift stores and ordinary shopping centers. The worst example is Yves St. Laurent's "Opium" perfume, manufactured by Squibb Pharmaceutical Company and marketed with drug-related advertising: a glossy ad exhorts the reader to enter the "Opium" world of fantasy and desires—a clear allusion to smoking opium. Thus, corporate exploitation of the drug culture is pushing the idea of drug intoxication. The Florida Pediatric Society has voted to boycott all Squibb pharmaceutical products if it does not change the advertising for "Opium" perfume. This action follows three years of protest from medical groups and parents which the company simply shrugged off.

If you are raising children today you must feel a sense of urgency. Children are experiencing something that no other generation in world history has gone through. They live in a society that has forgotten to protect children from predatory merchandising and commercial manipulation. The cleverest and most effective advertising and marketing strategies are being designed to take advantage of normal adolescent insecurity.

I think this merchandising of drugs to kids is a new problem. All of you have been working for years with alcoholism; many of you have been working for years with drugs. But only since about 1976 has the lid been taken off what merchants are doing to sell to kids. Alan Blum, who founded "Doctors Ought to Care"—a maverick group of street guerillas made up of medical students and interns who counteradvertise on cigarette billboards—calls his presentations "How the Corporate Pushers Keep on Truckin' After the Kids." He shows how the soft drink industry, the wine industry, the tobacco industry, and other corporations are getting kids onto "starter drugs"—cigarettes, beer, and pop wines—which we know have links with illicit drug-abuse behavior.

You cannot isolate one product from the other. This is how the kids begin—these are what my husband calls the "training bras of drug abuse."

Practical Parental Action

Many teachers and parents working in the alcohol- and drug-abuse field are optimistic about the changes we have seen in the past few years since parents started organizing, educating themselves, and trying to work more effectively with other groups. The parents' effort has not always been easy. Quite often there have been battles with agencies and professionals. But a more and more constructive coalition is developing.

We all have to recognize that adolescence is a very special time. We cannot treat teenagers as little children, using naive prevention strategies. We cannot treat them as adults because they are in a vulnerable period of internal stress, confusion, and irrationality. They are particularly vulnerable because of their tendency to be more loyal to their friends than to their own welfare. Kids are much more afraid of losing friends than of using drugs; this is something parents have had a very hard time learning.

But what do kids care more about than Opium perfume, Visine ads in *Seventeen* magazine, Schlitz beer, etc.? First, they care about their bodies. They want to be attractive to their peers; hence all that preening in front of the mirror, the endless showers, all the irritations parents go through with 13- or 14-year-olds. Young adolescents are utterly insecure about whether they are normal and attractive. Second, they care about access to automobiles, which carry an aura of freedom and fun. Third, they care about working out a rewarding relationship with their parents. Finally, they want to know how to deal with peer pressure.

In teaching parents how to teach their children about alcohol and drugs we have found it best to tell them about the biology of pleasure, what it means, and how it can be short circuited. This covers the role that the brain's reward system plays in motivation, the desire for achievement, self-discipline, etc. This may sound difficult, but we find that children and adolescents are fascinated to learn that things that feel good—food, sex, physical exertion, etc.—may have a function in terms of survival and the ability to protect oneself and one's family. The biological aspects can be a positive part of prevention, because in an age of physical fitness mania, people are very interested in their bodies—particularly 12- to 14-year-olds whose bodies seem to be giving them a lot of trouble.

Parents' groups and voluntary educational groups in the communities really need more information on the physiological effects of alcohol and drugs on children who are still growing. We need new information on developmental problems of puberty, on the reproductive system, muscle structure, and bone structure. This has been our most effective educational strategy. Yet five years ago, when we tried to get information on how the depletion of testosterone caused by marijuana may affect a 14-year-old boy at a time when his voice is changing and his muscles are developing, we could not get it anywhere. We had to go to amateurs and then to researchers and doctors in other fields to help us put this profile together. Despite what we were seeing right before our eyes—thin-waisted, undeveloped young boys—we could still not get anyone in the research field to say it was real. Clinical reports are only now beginning to appear in the pediatric literature.

We need alcohol information that applies to adolescent and pubertal development. This is something kids are interested in, that their parents can talk to them about. What goes on when your voice changes or your breasts begin to develop? What changes go on in your body that chemicals may disrupt? It is an unemotional way to talk about problems that have been very difficult and embarrassing to discuss. We need help— we cannot get enough of this information. All over the country, mothers have been trying to read medical journals, trying to find out why the information they need is not available when millions of kids are using alcohol and drugs. We get very little help from the medical and research community in this area; there is a tremendous information gap.

The parent movement started out on the drug issue, which scared parents more than the alcohol issue because they did not understand it. We began by trying to get parents to face their responsibility for their children's health, to ask their children: What are the risks you are taking for the future of your own children? Is it worth taking a chance that someday this drug use may show up in an unhealthy offspring or some kind of genetic problem? The health approach also has immediate appeal: parents, teachers, coaches, or pediatricians can talk to youngsters about what a healthy body is. Parents are responsible for their children's health and make the rules about vaccination, measles, and everything else medical; they should make it about drugs and alcohol. We try to teach parents why these drugs are more physiologically harmful to someone who is not physically mature. This approach avoids having to get into psychoanalysis, into emotional judgments such as saying to teenagers that they are not mature yet. Most kids believe they are mature at 12—they will admit that sixth graders are not mature, but they believe that seventh graders are.

A very important element in our strategy is for parents to link up in networks or with peer groups. These parent support groups, which can be very loose and informal or quite organized, are able to say: "Regardless of the media, regardless of what is on television, regardless of what is for sale at the nearby store, we will maintain around our children a mutual code that stipulates what is permissible behavior." Such a code does not have to cover everything, but it should cover illegal activity, the use of drugs and alcohol, getting into dangerous situations with automobiles, etc. It should be based on common sense. The most disparate types of parents—atheists and Baptists, liberals and conservatives—can agree on essential areas of risk, and then build a mini-society around their children that has a different standard of behavior, a different standard of what is tolerated, than the trashy commercial culture. Parents can stick together and support each other.

The process is simple, it is a matter of reinventing the wheel, but it works because the main thing by which kids judge their own behavior is what their friends are allowed to do. In situations of divorce, of working parents, etc., the parental network is a godsend; it gives a person 15 other parents to work with to raise a batch of kids. The parents can help each other and swap places at times. If mothers cannot be home in the afternoons—single, working mothers particularly have a hard time with this—they can call on neighbors, other people in the network to say, "Can my kids come check in at your house?" The process does work—it is very practical.

We have found that parents need to understand the health and developmental risks that children face when they experiment with drugs and alcohol. It is not something to waffle about. Parents are trying to help them mature and become independent and leave home—that is the whole point. The kids need to know that, too. The specter we hold out to the teenagers is this: "What if you become a burn-out or an alcoholic, still living with your mother, getting an allowance, when you are 28?" We present the ultimate nightmare to the parents: "What if they come home when they are 28 because they are immature and can't make it? What if you end up with a burnt out, permanent adolescent on your hands?" There are consequences to the misuse of pleasurable chemicals that are not just a matter of hitting someone with a car, but of a young person's ability to develop capacities for controlling impulses in a way that is constructive and can lead to a productive life.

Teenage Parties and Parental Responsibility

I want finally to address the question of adult legal liability in relation to underage drinking. The 16-year-old male driver is statistically the biggest killer on the highway; the glands reach their height of activity at the same time the kid gets a gearshift in his hand—it is not a very rational period. The laws on underage drinking are too often not enforced by parents, police, merchants, or even medical personnel such as emergency room crews and ambulance drivers. In my own community in Atlanta, where for many years prevention efforts went nowhere because anything entailing the slightest restriction of individual choice was immediately backed away from—even when kids were stoned at school or drunk on the highways—what finally got through to parents was their legal liability.

What we say in PTA meetings and such is the following. First, there are good, sound, medical reasons for the laws on underage drinking—the physiology of puberty makes the kids vulnerable; it is not the same to be 16 and drinking as to be 21 and drinking. Second, parents are responsible for the behavior of minors in their homes and under their supervision, whether their own children's or someone else's. If the daughter is having a slumber party and the parents are upstairs watching television, the kids get drunk from bottles out of the liquor cabinet and one of them drives away and kills someone, it is the host parents' responsibility. If they did not know it was going on, that is neglect in the supervision of minors. Even for the libertarian parents in our community, this made sense. Even the kids thought it made sense; at the PTA forums they asked us incredible lawyer's questions: "Well, what if the parents were asleep and we all got drunk, is it still their fault?" The answer is "Yes"; parents are responsible for the safety and welfare of the kids in their home or on their property. The point made the teenagers recognize their own responsibility not to get parents in trouble. This is a tremendous public message.

The typical high school party now is a completely unsupervised scene of very heavy drinking. It begins in about the seventh grade. By ninth grade, kids feel they cannot give a birthday party without having drinks, because no one will come. Parents are buffaloed, and police often do nothing because that is what the community demands. I mention two recent, shocking episodes involving the kids from suburban Atlanta, from nice schools, good homes, etc.

First, a party was held when someone's parents were out of town. The word went out at the high school and the kids all flocked there—a nice big house, a doctor's family. A boy who was never in trouble with alcohol before got drunk. His girlfriend got mad at him, he lost control, and knocked her down the stairs. She became paralyzed. The kids, all about 14-16 years old, panicked and called the emergency room. The ambulance came, the attendants revived the girl, decided she was not permanently damaged, and drove away—from a household of teenage drunks. The crew never made a record. The house, with some 200 drunk kids partying in it, was trashed. The incident was completely covered up until some of the kids grew concerned because the girl was still having back trouble and her parents did not know what had happened.

Two weeks later there was an incident involving two more teenage parties. The parents were not home at one and were upstairs at the other; there was heavy drinking at both parties. The police were called by the neighbors to the first party four times. They told the 16-year-old teenage host, "Cool it, the neighbors are mad at you," and went on. The kids from that party went to another party; there was a fight between football team members of different schools; a boy who was not drinking tried to break up the fight, was stabbed six times and died. The host parents were upstairs and had no idea there had been a fight until the boy bled to death in their living room. This is nice, suburban, good-family America.

In these instances the parents were either upstairs or absent, yet they were legally liable. That may seem cruel if they were unaware of the law and their responsibility, but they should not have been unaware. The police and paramedics did not expect community support, so they took no strong preventive action, even in cases of violence and injury. These are the realities of what we are dealing with. The widespread adolescent drug and alcohol problem is urgent and unprecedented—we should remember that. The sophisticated marketing of intoxicants to children has never happened before, especially not at the accelerating rates of the last few years. But the parental instinct to protect a child's physical well-being is the strongest instinct in nature and in society. If we can tap that instinct and reinforce it with community support and legal sanctions, we can build an effective prevention movement.

WHAT SCHOOLS CAN DO: A PHILADELPHIA STORY

SISTER MADELEINE BOYD, Shalom, Inc.

I first entered the field of drug and alcohol abuse as a school disciplinarian, responsible for the behavior problems of 3,000 girls in a school in Philadelphia's Little Italy. Though my background was in guidance, administration, and psychology, I had always had children with behavior problems, mainly because I was always bigger than they were. My first drug case confused me because I thought that my 6-foot-tall, German-Irish demeanor would make her stop and think twice—it usually did. But the drug-prone adolescent was a bird of a different feather. She would look at me with cocker spaniel eyes and I would believe anything she said—until I was burnt once, twice, but never a third time.

I realized I needed an education in how to communicate with these children, how to understand their game. They had to be liars because drugs were illegal. I took off for a summer, and for a religious, taking a summer off is like asking for four years of sabbatical. I visited every nearby drug and alcohol program to see which ones I could trust with the lives of my girls. When I returned I had a pretty good evaluation of which programs I would send girls to, but I also wondered, what am I and the other teachers in the schools going to do about this? Treatment was a great resource. Much of my work would be preparation for treatment, support during treatment, and support after treatment—but treatment comes after the child is already scarred. What about prevention? We needed to give students some weapons and skills to handle their own problems and make their own decisions. Most important, we needed to give them the truth. In the early 1970s there were volumes of absolutely wrong information about drugs. Gradually, the students became so sophisticated in their use of drugs that they turned to alcohol because it was easier and safer and involved less pressure from the adult world. I thought we had an obligation or responsibility to gain knowledge, skills, strategies, and techniques to face this problem honestly and communicate with the children. As an educator I saw a need to reach children before they were scarred.

I hear a lot of rhetoric about prevention but I do not see many green bucks coming into this field. While I respect the idea and the contributions of volunteerism in prevention, I believe we also need professionals who are well instructed in psychology, social work, guidance techniques, life-planning skills, etc. There the government is deficient. It comes through at times, but only after treatment has received the lion's share. What is left over, treated as a luxury, is prevention.

The principal reason my program got drug and alcohol money from the state was the fear that high school children were becoming involved in criminal behavior. Legislatures respond more readily to criminal offenses and to anything connected with criminal justice; the government is pressured more strongly to stop crime than to help human growth. So I told the government of Pennsylvania that I resented the fact that they pay 175 dollars a day for a child who is incarcerated, and 0.3 cents to prevent him or her from becoming incarcerated.

It was a long, hard job, but with support from teachers, parents, and students, I was able to flesh out my skeleton of an idea and gradually develop the program, Shalom. We began our program in the schools by hiring people who had professional life-training skills. They were social workers, psychologists, and guidance counselors, who had a way of communicating with teenagers. Our program now operates in 15 high schools, 22 grammar schools, and 3 counties, and we have 5 men out on the streets from 2-10 pm doing work in the community.

To communicate with children we first had to gain rapport with them. We had to know what they were reading, what they were listening to, what they were seeing on television and in the movies, and what their language communicated. This was and is a prerequisite to understanding why, where, with whom, and in what places they drink and what attracts them to drinking and drugs. The kids know alcohol is socially accepted. They feel not only peer pressure but also social pressure. What scene on television does not have a decanter and wine glasses? At present, alcoholism in youth is a terrific problem—even for 10-year-olds.

We start our program in the high schools, where there is a captive audience. The program is not in the health class curriculum. It is offered during study periods and before and after school. It is a highly structured discussion group from which they can learn new skills and at the same time gain new knowledge, techniques, and strategies to implement this knowledge. The facts are presented in various ways: through psycho-drama, magazines, music, videotapes, and movies. It is not labeled "drug education." It is labeled "personal awareness" or "leadership training"—everyone wants to be a leader.

We give kids the truth about all the ramifications of drinking and taking drugs. Then we can say: "If you are still willing to take the risk and you gamble and lose, then you can cry on your own shoulder." This spring we have been showing the movie "The Last Prom," so that the kids would see all the possible problems created by drinking before the prom: "You can get messed up with the law, with your insurance, with dad's car, with the girl's family—so if you take the risk, you make an informed choice."

If we give information to teenagers in a rational way and give them the skills to discuss it openly, we will not only whip drugs and alcohol, but all sorts of problematic behavior. We are now dealing with rape, incest, homosexuality, and child abuse, networking to bring in other agencies to help deal with these problems. We have to communicate the dignity of the child to the child—make it known that he or she is valuable, lovable, and that his or her health is a primary consideration and most essential. There is no need for drugs and alcohol, for kids can learn to get high on life.

RESEARCH APPROACHES TO PRIMARY PREVENTION

ALFRED MCALISTER, University of Texas Health Sciences Center

Primary prevention of alcohol abuse is among the great modern public health challenges. Society is eager for ideas about how to communicate with children and young people to reduce or deter the irresponsible use of alcohol. There are two basic educational approaches to the prevention of youthful alcohol abuse. One can be labeled "direct" or "specific," in that it represents direct efforts specifically concerned with alcohol. A contrasting approach can be termed "indirect" or "general," as it refers to efforts intended to have a general, indirect impact on a number of different behavioral threats to health. I will illustrate each approach with studies by research teams.

Direct, Specific Prevention Approaches

The most direct approaches to prevention are proscriptions enforced by harsh punitive systems, or the promise of hellish consequences. American political philosophy, however, is based on the notion of voluntary self-restraint; we do not impose harsh restrictions and punishments to control alcohol abuse as do Moslem societies, for example. Moral approbations also seem to have lost much of their force in our secular society. Pursuing the ideal of enlightenment, educators have in recent years appealed to young people's capacity for rational decision, providing straight, factual information about alcohol and its effects. These efforts have yielded disappointing results (Gordon and McAlister, 1982). While leading to increased knowledge and understanding, factual alcohol education has not appeared to have much impact on behavior.

The most recent preventive efforts have been concerned less with enlightment than with motivation. Peer pressure is a widely recognized motive for adolescents' risk-taking behavior (Sherif and Sherif, 1974), and efforts to create positive peer influences and interfere with negative peer influences have shown promising results in the prevention of adolescent cigarette smoking (Evans et al., 1979). In research undertaken first at Stanford and then at Harvard University, I have evaluated the effects of peer programs for alcohol and other substance abuse prevention.

In the Stanford study, peer leaders about age 16 led 12-year-old students in sessions designed to reduce the perceived social desirability of cigarette smoking, frequent marijuana use, and drunkenness. In the follow-up, self-reports of drunkenness were significantly less frequent among students in the program than among those in a control school

(McAlister et al., 1980). In a more recent study, students in inner-city schools in Boston were randomly assigned either to a peer program that opposed specific substance use or to serve as a comparison population. Of 16 classroom hours of special substance abuse prevention activity spread across 2 years of junior high or middle school, 7 hours were concerned with alcohol. Of 6 sessions involving peer-nominated "opinion leaders," 3 contained material concerned with alcohol. A variety of educational approaches was included. For example, a videotape was produced in which an on-screen character attempted to persuade the viewer to engage in a drinking contest. Counterarguments were scrolled across the bottom of the screen so that by reading the lines the viewer experienced the illusion of interpersonal communication. The most popular students in each classroom were chosen to read the responses, followed by a group reading. The script was designed to promote the perception that heavy drinking was socially undesirable.

Although the frequencies of self-reported drinking at monthly or shorter intervals were comparable at baseline, there were sharp differences between comparison and experimental groups in reported alcohol abuse at follow-up, which suggests that a preventive effect was achieved. Differences between cohorts are presented in Table 6-1. These results are not definitive: only about half the students eligible for longitudinal study are represented; the treatment and control schools had different attrition rates; and there were serious inconsistencies in program delivery, severely limiting confidence in inferring a preventive effect. Nevertheless, at least some part of the differences can be attributed to the preventive program. More rigorous experimental research is needed to determine just how effective a short-term preventive strategy has been developed.

Indirect, General Preventive Approaches

Long-term patterns of alcohol abuse may be determined more by the larger social environment than by immediate peer pressure. A variety of evidence links alcohol abuse with factors such as disruptions in family or community relationships. If such factors cause a broad range of detrimental behaviors, then these factors should be addressed by preventive efforts, even though they are resistant to modification.

In research on general, indirect approaches to primary prevention, the most important studies may be ones that seek to improve social skills, family relations, and school attendance and achievement. Few investigators have been bold enough to intervene in these difficult areas. The stimulating reports of Bry (1982) and Bry and George (1980) suggest

TABLE 6-1   Percentage of Frequent Alcohol Users at Baseline and
Follow-up in Treatment and Control Cohorts

	Start of 6th Grade	End of 7th Grade	
	Monthly or More Frequent Drinking	Monthly or More Frequent Drinking	Monthly or More Frequent Drunkenness
Treatment (n = 140)	11.4	7.1[a]	3.6[b]
Control (n = 105)	12.4	25.7	14.3

[a]$x^2 = 15.8$, p < .001.
[b]$x^2 = 9.2$, p < .001.

that intensive efforts to improve school attendance and achievement
may be successful, but the small number of subjects and the short time-
span of these and related studies weaken confidence in their implications. Other studies have attempted to improve family relationships
(Pratt, 1976) or individual characteristics such as self-esteem (Botvin
et al., 1980), but no clear-cut findings have yet been obtained from well-
controlled studies. The progress of research in this area is limited by
difficulties in conceptualization; family and community life appear to
be influenced by differences among individuals, but the personal attri-
butes most central to the quality of human experience have not been
isolated.

It may be impossible to improve family and school relationships on
any significant scale under conditions of high unemployment or other
social stress and deterioration. Despite the magnitude of such pressing
structural problems, they are not necessarily beyond the scope of social-
psychological analysis or intervention on a small-scale basis. Small-
scale changes may produce only short-term results, but they can provide
evidence for the potential and possibility of change.

In a recent study, an effort was made to investigate the short-term
psychological impact of altering an important structural variable: eighth-
grade students in an inner-city, minority setting of high youth unemployment, where the number of government-sponsored summer jobs
had been sharply cut, were randomly assigned to be eligible for enhanced
summer employment opportunities related to long-term career goals.
At the beginning and end of the school year the assigned students
completed an interview that measured future orientation, self-esteem,
and coping styles.

Experimental subjects participated in a series of weekly classroom
sessions and field trips designed to increase social support and self-

esteem and to improve coping skills. The summer jobs were a salient part of the intervention: there was evidence of short-term increased attendance when special job eligibility forms were issued. Self-esteem was enhanced by direct social approval and by identification of each individual's positive qualities. Coping skills were taught by actual problem solving in small groups in which students were urged to express their most pressing problems, to discuss solutions, and to apply those solutions experimentally. All sessions were led by a group of Harvard undergraduates with cultural backgrounds similar to the study participants.

Group differences in self-reports about relevant variables are presented in Table 6-2. At follow-up with about two-thirds of the participants, the experimental subjects tended to display more positive future orientation and greater self-efficacy. These experimental methods and short-term findings may not be generalizable or stable, but the data point toward future, more substantial studies.

Implications

There are many conferences on smoking, heart disease, cancer, and similar disease-specific or substance-specific issues. In these meetings, 95-98 percent of the discussion involves the policies or actions that might be addressed to specific problems, without looking at broader, underlying matters. If one points out that unemployment causes families to break up, and when families break up, wider disruptions happen, such as not using hypertensive medication, not quitting smoking, not controlling alcohol use, and so on, everyone will agree and then drop the subject.

Similarly, one can point out that the overall quality of education in the schools is fundamental. How can a school mount an effective alcohol abuse program unless it has adequate funding, unless the teachers are paid well enough that the social climate in the school is not "I hate this place," but "This is a good place to be"? If one says the fundamental problem is the quality of schools and the amount of money that we as a society invest in our children and their socialization, everyone may agree—but nothing comes of it.

I do not think we can reach our long-term goals without building coalitions that cut across all these specific concerns, bringing along those whose lives are touched by alcohol, by smoking, and so forth. I want to illustrate this with one specific example. In Texas the governor has promised teachers a pay raise and he is committed to improving the overall quality of education. In order to fund that pay raise, he wants

TABLE 6-2   Follow-up Group Differences in Future Orientation and
Self-Efficacy

	Experimental	Control
	n (percent)	
Future Orientation		
Do you look forward to your future?		
Yes	27(90)[a]	18(58)
Undecided	3(10)	9(29)
No	0(0)	4(13)
Self-Efficacy		
Could you do something about a recent problem?[b]		
Yes	15(65)[c]	12(52)
Undecided	6(26)	2(9)
No	2(9)	9(39)

[a]$p < .05$ by Kolmogorov-Smirnov test.
[b]Among those reporting a recent problem.
[c]$p < .10$ by Kolmogorov-Smirnov test.

to increase alcohol and cigarette taxes. No one has yet drawn the
connection that if the overall quality of schooling improves, maybe that
will help prevent adolescent alcohol abuse, smoking, and other such
problems. The people in the state who are concerned with alcohol sit
on the sidelines asking, "What does the teachers' pay raise have to do
with alcohol problems?" I think that it is important to make this kind
of connection explicit.

It would be terribly misleading to say, "Let us look just at the quality
of education," and forget regulatory laws and prevention curricula and
other alcohol-specific measures, but I think we should invest something
more than 2-5 percent of our effort in these more general problems, and
I do not think we will build successful coalitions for prevention until
we do that.

PREVENTING DRUNK DRIVING

Edward Kunec, Mothers Against Drunk Drivers

I am not in this field as a professional but because some 21 months
ago my wife and I lost a 20-year-old son, killed by a 19-year-old drunk
driver. I became affiliated with Mothers Against Drunk Drivers (MADD),
an association of mothers, fathers, sons, daughters, friends, and relatives. The organization has blossomed in 3 years as a result of a national

tragedy that affects every one of us. Currently, MADD has 153 chapters in 38 states; to establish a MADD chapter requires at least 20 people who are committed to writing letters, meeting with local political leaders, speaking before organizations, and trying to elicit public sympathy and action.

My chapter is made up of 100 dues-paying members and 100 others who contribute in one way or another to our efforts. Our organization receives no outside funding—it is all volunteer help—and as a result, our resources and our help are limited. Within the limits of the resources that we have, we do try to look at things from a system perspective and to cover as many of the elements as we can.

We have discussed the overall problem with local officials. Alcohol is not just a problem of the young—it covers all age groups. But our sheriff indicates that approximately 80 percent of those in jail in my county are under the age of 30, and most of the problems they have are alcohol- and drug-related. This 80 percent figure is mind-boggling.

We have tried to make the local community aware of the drunk-driving problem through news media exposure, through television, through schools, and in speaking with our friends and neighbors before organizations like the Kiwanis, the Lions, the PTA, etc. We have thus far successfully persuaded five county governments in Virginia to form task forces comprised of civic leaders, public officials, and interested citizens, to study their local problem and their resources to cope with it and to make recommendations for public and private action. We successfully encouraged the governor of Virginia, Charles Robb, to form a task force at the state level. We have encouraged legislative change, which is one of the most difficult things we have encountered and on which we need a great deal of assistance. We have encouraged better enforcement of our laws, which is also very difficult in Virginia because the judges are appointed by the legislature and somehow feel beholden to that body instead of to the people in the community. That is one of our most difficult problems on the local level—to encourage judges to pass sentences to the full extent of the law.

For example, we were recently appalled to learn that an individual who drunkenly killed a young woman with his automobile in 1978, when he was a juvenile (for which reason, nothing happened to him), has subsequently been arrested on five infractions related to drunk driving. His attorney has, in our view, subverted the intent of the law, using the legal system such that the individual has served not one day in jail. The legal system simply has not provided the necessary and just sanctions. Because of a newspaper article on this case, the commonwealth's attorney in this jurisdiction has instituted a grand jury hearing; possibly some reasonable justice will now be imposed.

We feel that our local court systems, although fair, could do their job in a more just way. One of the biggest problems is continuance of trials, that is, delay from the originally scheduled day the trial was to take place, for weeks, months, or years, while the defendant shops for a more sympathetic judge or a lesser plea. Depending on the jurisdiction, between one-third and one-half of all trials are continued.

If such an appalling degree of absenteeism existed in our school system, we would call it a tragedy. It is a national tragedy that the whim of the defense can gain a continuance, and that our prosecuting attorneys and court system allow this. I am outraged at our current system after seeing how it operates. I know in my heart that something needs to be done. The problem in the past has been a lack of community support at the local level. This is the key: the more people become knowledgeable about this problem, the better off our communities will be.

COMMENTS ON ALCOHOL, YOUTH, AND DRUNK DRIVING

FRANK RAFLO, County of Loudoun, Virginia

In light of the many suggestions for using the law to control the problems we have been discussing, I would particularly like to know what the evidence is on whether restrictive measures on individuals, or the fear of punishment for the abuse of alcohol and possible crimes resulting from it, have any impact on the use of alcohol. We are a nation that says, "Put them in jail." We also say, "We do not want to pay any more money for jails, rehabilitation, or courts." Under these circumstances, do punitive measures or the fear of punishment have any impact on lessening the abuse of alcohol?

CLAY HALL, National Highway Traffic Safety Administration

We do not know if fear of punishment has any impact on reduction of consumption. We are seeing some results in terms of drunk driving. Where we are increasing the fear of arrest and the general deterrence aspect using fines, licensing action, etc., these actions are having some impact in reducing alcohol-related fatal and injury crashes. The biggest problem nationally is that we still do not have a sufficient fear of punishment—we can create it for a short time, but people soon perceive that the courts are not really fining people or taking licenses away; it is a paper tiger. Some communities are turning this around; in Maryland, for example, there has been good public information, good enforcement, and significant reductions in nighttime fatal crashes. We are at least changing the attitude in some communities such that drunks are not getting behind the wheel of a car. I do not know whether they are drinking any less, but they are not driving when they do.

MARK MOORE, Harvard University

Are we in the grip of a struggle over restrictive policies? Is there not some middle ground or different front that can be opened to somehow make that tension, which nearly everyone seems to feel, between individual license on one hand and paternalistic restrictiveness on the other, a little less sharp? What public spirit is out there that makes it easy or attractive to pass repressive measures—which, after all, will turn out to cost a great deal of money in the form of jail capacity and required treatment?

MARILYN GOLDWATER, Maryland House of Delegates

In today's climate in state legislatures, at least in the Maryland legislature, it is politically easier to pass legislation that deals with punitive aspects of problems than to pass legislation that deals with education or, particularly when you have tight budgets, provides funds for the type of programs that educate people and change public attitudes. That is where the public pressure comes from; the other kind of pressure is there and is increasing, but it is not nearly as strong. In the same way, sometimes it is easier to pass legislation in the capital budget, which builds a building you can point to, than to find money in the operating budget to provide the programs and services necessary to make that building do what it is intended to do.

Of course, punitive or restrictive measures are not all that easy to legislate. For example, no Maryland law prohibits drinking while you drive. I proposed legislation for several years, before finally giving up, that would prohibit open bottles of alcohol in the car. There were all kinds of interesting reactions. "If I am in the middle of mowing my lawn and run out of beer and drive to the local store to get some more and take a sip when I get into my car on the way home, can I get arrested?" Or let us say you wanted to make a law to permit carrying an open bottle of alcohol from the house to the beach or to a picnic, as long as the bottle was in a concealed part of the car, like the trunk;

unfortunately, some cars do not have a trunk or other place to put something so that the driver and passengers cannot get at it.

People come to the legislature and say, "This is a problem in my community; let us get it solved." They look at it as very simple, but to draft a piece of workable legislation and get consensus on it is very difficult. Sometimes we can get consensus only on a piece of empty legislation.

ROBERT REYNOLDS, County of San Diego

There is a lack of comparability in the clarity of the alternatives we have been discussing. It is easy for legislators to understand punishment and treatment; it is difficult to understand prevention. If you spend money on prevention, how do you measure the results? We are not able at this point to give clear enough recommendations to legislative bodies on what is an efficient use of resources. I think it is both the climate of the times as well as the status of our research and knowledge that is preventing us from moving forward. We are simply not able to speak clearly on the directions in which we should move forward, particularly in the face of some rather grim research on some historic prevention efforts.

MARK MOORE, Harvard University

When we take official, government-sponsored, authorized action with budgets and laws attached to it, there is a special need for simplicity, and maybe it comes out a little punitive because that fits with what people think the government is capable of doing. That would be one way to think about it. And yet we have heard eloquent accounts of unofficial, nongovernmental enterprises, which seem to have a lot of force behind them as well as a great deal of sensitivity to detail, so that the force is exercised in a careful and discreet way by volunteer groups. I have a general kind of view that all of these things turn out to be more complementary than we are inclined to think, that public and private work together, that punitive and treatment approaches work together, that taxation and education work together, that all the things that we imagine as being starkly opposite, as representing alternative routes, gain power when we put them together.

KEITH SCHUCHARD, Parental Resource Institute for Drug Education

Laws work best when they represent the concerns of citizens. I think most drunk-driving laws, for example, which we call punitive (I do not think that has to have negative connotations; it means that we publicly define something as wrong and therefore apply a legal penalty), work when there has been enough education in the community to arouse the concern of the people who will be affected and who are willing to vote those laws in. Mothers Against Drunk Drivers got laws passed that many legislators hated because so many of them drink and drive. It was a very difficult lobbying effort.

Prevention education for youth is a nebulous area. It comes into play somewhere between the naiveté and idealism of preteens—who believe their parents and like their teachers—and norms of responsible use for adults. In between there are mixed-up, muddy messages going to the adolescent, who is supposed to become adult and responsible in handling intoxicating chemicals that basically make him or her irresponsible. This is a very difficult area for the government to get involved in. Parents are legally responsible for their minor children's behavior and they are really the only ones who can make much difference. I do not think there has to be a dichotomy between legislative and voluntary approaches, but I think that forces that work on a large scale must fit in with the actual concerns of people most directly connected to the problem.

SHEILA BLUME, National Council on Alcoholism

Most people do not realize that the best data we have on public policy for alcohol problems relate specifically to the effect that changing the minimum legal purchase age has on road accidents. The studies indicate that the minimum purchase age does not stop teenagers from drinking but does powerfully influence where they drink. Data charts I have seen recently from a longitudinal study at Rutgers showed that below age 18 (the legal drinking age when this study cohort reached 18), the bar-drinking column was empty; above that age, the bar-drinking column had big numbers in it. The purchase age seems to determine when young people go to on-premise drinking sites in large numbers, and that influences road accidents. It also presumably affects the degree of control that parents can exercise over adolescents' drinking practices.

ROBERT STRAUS, University of Kentucky

The strongest argument that came out of the 1950s for lowering the drinking age in the first place was based on available data suggesting that in areas in which drinking was restricted fewer people drank; those who did, however, drank more, and the prevalence of drinking problems was much greater. College data were used as well as comparisons of consumption patterns and problems in local-option states. By the time implementation of the lower drinking age occurred in the early 1970s, based of course mainly on the shift in the voting age, we were in a completely different era with respect to intoxicant use in the United States.

I have been a bit concerned with the extent to which we may apply rather simplistic explanations to the apparent rise in problems due to the change in drinking age, without taking into account about six other things that were happening in society at the same time, such as the generalized increase in consumption of alcohol, the increase in use of a whole variety of substances by younger people, the enormous increase in the number of vehicles licensed to and driven by younger people, and several others.

PHILIP COOK, Duke University

A general social science research principle that is relevant here is that you have to actually try something to know whether it works the way you expect it to. And even then you will never know whether it works unless you intervene in a way that lends itself to assessment and make sure that someone is actually positioned to do the necessary research. That quasi-experimental situation occurred after the drinking age was lowered in many states in the early 1970s.

BARRY SWEEDLER, National Transportation Safety Board

The National Transportation Safety Board has made recommendations based on that research. While our recommendations are not mandatory and we have no enforcement authority, they have a high level of credibility and are usually given careful consideration, focusing national attention on what we consider to be important transportation safety issues.

We were particularly concerned about the problem of youth in traffic accidents, since about 20 percent of all fatal accidents involve drivers under the age of 21, while less than 10 percent of licensed drivers are in this age group. We felt this overrepresentation needed our attention. We considered the evidence very strong that raising the drinking age to 21 would help the problem of youth/alcohol/driving. I stress that this is not a total solution, but one that we felt had been proven indisputably effective by statistical analyses.

About 5,000 lives are lost each year in alcohol-related accidents in which the drivers are under 21. On the basis of the studies that have been done, we felt that about 1,250 lives, most of them young ones, could be saved each year if each state raised its drinking age to 21. With that information and a synopsis of all the research that we were familiar with, we addressed public recommendations to the governors and legislative leaders of 35 states (and the District of Columbia) that had a drinking age of less than 21 for some or all alcoholic beverages. These recommendations were made in July 1982, and support for them has come from across the board: the highway safety community, parents' groups, police groups, medical and insurance groups, the Bartenders Union, the President, the Secretary of Transportation, the Secretary of Health and Human Services. Congress has urged states to do this. The Gallup poll has shown that 77 percent of the population supports legislation to raise the drinking age to 21. Surprisingly, 58 percent of the youngsters in the affected age group, 18- to 20-year-olds, support this legislation. In almost every affected state, relevant legislation has been introduced; 4 states have raised the drinking age to 21, 3 other states to 19, and 1 to 20.

Whenever a proposal to raise the drinking age has been voted on by a legislative body in this country, it has not lost. But in many states it has been bottled up in committee, primarily because of strong lobbying efforts by people who sell alcohol primarily to youth, such as certain tavern owners. Citizens in a number of states have become disgusted with their own legislative process and have gone to the ballot initiative, where that is available. Michigan passed the proposition with a 58 percent majority. In Ohio, proponents are collecting signatures. In Arizona, the campaign was headed by a conservative Republican and a liberal Democrat, and the governor signed the first petition.

If the legislative bottlenecks on this issue were brought before the public through the media, the public that supports the change would put enough pressure on their legislators to force a vote.

MARK MOORE, Harvard University

I would like to ask Deputy Chief Kenny of the New York City Police what their experience has been with respect to the enforcement of some of these drunk-driving laws.

JOHN KENNY, New York City Police Department

In 1982 we made over 4,200 arrests for driving while intoxicated. About 52 percent were involved in accidents. The figures are not all up-to-date, but 83 percent of the chemical tests taken were at the 0.10

blood alcohol content level or higher (19 percent of the people refused to take the test). We were able to look at only 1,832 out of the 4,000-odd arrests, but we found an 83 percent conviction rate with an average fine of $234.00. We also found a lot of misdemeanor arrests—the violator pleaded to the lesser charge of driving-while-ability-impaired. A total of 4,281 arrests may not seem like many for New York City, but this was a 51 percent increase over 1981. The priority for driving-while-intoxicated has not been very high; we have problems with robberies and crimes against the person that have a much higher priority. But we are now putting more people into this; we want to do a better job.

In 1981 a law was passed in Albany, New York, providing that 50 percent of the fines collected as a result of driving-while-intoxicated arrests could be returned to the county in which the arrest was made for education, rehabilitation, and enforcement. So in May 1982 we started a very small, token program: We had 18 officers working Friday and Saturday nights between 6:00 pm and 4:00 am. We made 800 arrests with this program from May 1982 until May 1983. Of the 800 arrests, 93 percent were made by observation only—people not involved in accidents. It is a good program; we will get the money back; the only problem is that everyone is looking to get a piece of the money, and it comes back only after we have arrested the drunk driver. It is too late then. We should try to reach these people with education and rehabilitation before the police get to them; we wind up with them in family fights, child-battering incidents, accidents, and murders, as well as driving while intoxicated.

MARK MOORE, Harvard University

It seems to me that these two instruments are not separate. There is educational value associated with having the law and the arrests. In fact, the power of the educational effort is strengthened when you can say that the legislature decided that this is a bad level of drinking, that the risk of arrest for it is going up, and regardless of whether you think it is wise for you as an individual to drink and drive, this is what the law and other people think. The law and education seem to have potentiating effects—one helping the other. And the law itself has enormous educational power.

CHARLES CRAWFORD, Gallo Winery

I think that we should focus on encouraging social responsibility among young people and not on trying to force prevention on anyone. Let me illustrate this. During Prohibition, the town I lived in was 80 percent Italian, and everyone drank wine. My family made the legal limit of wine, 200 gallons, each year. If we went to someone else's house, the jug of wine came out and everyone had a glass, including the children. There was no drunkenness on these occasions. I do not remember seeing anyone intoxicated all the time I grew up. But when I went to high school in 1932, we took a mandatory field trip to the closest jail, to see the drunk tank. That was the first time I had seen anybody drunk, and I will never forget it.

How can we encourage responsible behavior today? The Bible is probably the most-read book in the United States, but next—at least in California—is the official driver's license handbook. The California Driver's Handbook has two full pages about punitive sanctions on drunk driving but nothing on how much alcohol it takes to achieve a blood alcohol content (BAC) of 0.10 percent. The reader should learn that two glasses of wine over a mealtime period of 1-2 hours will not cause 0.10 percent BAC, while four beers consumed quickly to quench thirst on a hot day can put BAC over 0.10 percent. I know 18- and 19-year-olds who actually think they can drink a six-pack and drive better! If every driver's handbook had a few pages, not on punitive laws but on what causes drunk driving and what constitutes social responsibility, I think it would mean a lot.

The next most widely read documents are the newspaper and the comics. The Bureau of Alcohol, Tobacco, and Firearms put out a comic book on alcohol a couple of years ago that I thought quite effective. Something could be done in every Sunday comic, to catch kids who are 12-16 years old, who I do not say should not drink, but should drink temperately and understand that food and beverages go together.

Much can be done. I am on the Stanislaus County Advisory Board on Alcohol Problems. Drunk driving is down by 40 percent in Stanislaus County, but we see it slipping back up again, because people lose interest: the police lose interest, the judges have no more room to throw people in jail, and they start to forget about it. I try to stir them up again. I believe that social responsibility is the answer. In Stanislaus County right now we are using role playing to talk about drinking. One kid pretends he has a new car and a six-pack of beer; he picks up two friends, and they invent a dialogue—what do you say, what do you do if somebody says have a drink of beer? This approach works. If you give them a lecture, 50 percent do not even listen; when you get them doing it voluntarily, they become socially responsible.

JAY LEWIS, National Council on Alcoholism

Mr. Crawford, you would put messages about the social responsibilities involved in alcohol use on widely read materials like the driver's handbook. I wonder if you would put information related to the addictive quality of alcohol on the labels of wine bottles? I assume that purchasers of wine would be reading the labels.

CHARLES CRAWFORD, Gallo Winery

I wish that were true. Yet I watch my daughter smoke cigarettes, and you know what it says on the package of cigarettes. Warning labels on the bottles will not do any good at all. They might be read once and then forgotten. But applicants are going to be asked questions about their driver's license handbook, and if they miss a few of those questions, they will not get the license. Every day, thousands of people take that driver's license test.

DAN BEAUCHAMP, University of North Carolina

In North Carolina you only have to read the driver's handbook once every five years. I do not think that will be very helpful to us.

GAIL HEALY, White House Office of Drug Policy

We need to offer positive alternatives—natural highs—to young people, to combat the media and advertising campaigns to "take this substance and be superwoman or superman." I recently spent a weekend watching a meet of the U.S. white-water canoe team. The way of life they are dedicated to does not totally exclude alcohol, but their schedule does not give them time to become addicted. Young people are involved in ballet, in art, in music, in many things outside of "dedicated partying" of the sort that Keith Schuchard described.

MARK MOORE, Harvard University

I would take issue with the suggestion that the out-of-control teenage party leading to violence or injury is "typical." The problem is that it is not typical; it is an extreme event that happens in circumstances that are typical but that hardly ever produce the results that were described. For every 1,000 drunken teenage parties, or some number like that, there will be one that produces a broken limb. Certainly, the drunken party in some sense produces that injury, but it produces it probabilistically. Over a large enough group of people it is going to happen, but for each party it is a very unlikely event. How should we manage that? Not by banning teenage parties, but by managing them. As a parent, incidentally, I would be grateful for a law that gave me responsibility and set the community's standard, so that I would be in the position of enforcing the law and the standard with respect to my own house and children. I would take that responsibility seriously and I would know when I was well inside or outside that standard. The dilemma for us is that there are a lot of activities that sometimes, probabilistically, produce bad consequences, but mostly do not, and yet these probabilities call on us to exercise substantial managerial effort.

KEITH SCHUCHARD, Parental Resource Institute for Drug Education

Unfortunately, these cases are not as isolated as we might like to think. County and neighborhood newspapers carry local stories like this constantly. The problem is usually underreported, because the law does not get involved or these cases are not reported in the paper as drinking incidents.

DAVID KRAFT, University of Massachusetts, Amherst

The liability issue has been one of the things that got my prevention program moving into the university dormitories, because the dormitory managers were worried about their liability if something happened. This galvanized the students; they were worried that they were not going to be able to use alcohol at their parties at all, and we got a major change in party planning. I think liability can be used to good advantage, and circumstances in which people realize they might be responsible are important.

SISTER MADELEINE BOYD, Shalom, Inc.

Many parents ask us what to do about parties for their teenagers, who do not want to give a party unless there is beer. My answer is that the parents can be sued. For one's own child, one's own family, it is okay. But many people in Pennsylvania have been prosecuted when a child from another family was served beer with an adult present. This is a real-life deterrent in the home. If you serve somebody outside the family, you are legally liable.

MICHAEL FOX, Ohio General Assembly

The liability issue is very important to the question of making students take breathalyzer tests when suspected of being intoxicated or under the influence of alcohol. In my district in Ohio, when a principal thought that a high school student was involved with alcohol, he would send the student to the emergency room and ask that a blood test be done. Doctors did not want to deal with this because they had to have parental consent to give the test. As a result, the only results that the principal heard about were those that showed that the child did not have any alcohol or drugs in his or her body. If the test results did not come back the way the parents wanted them to, they faced the choice, "If I communicate the results of this test, my child will be expelled from school; if I do not tell them, my child may not learn a lesson." What is the doctor's liability? In the situation that Keith Schuchard mentioned involving the ambulance driver, did that person have the authority to shut that party down? Did he have any liability for *not* acting? The general point is that liability is a powerful tool, that it affects many situations in which alcohol is involved, and that a coordinated approach, drawing on the interests of a variety of groups, may be a solid base that can attract the workable coalitions necessary to get legislative action.

7 Community Cooperation to Reduce Alcohol Problems

ALTERING THE DRINKING ENVIRONMENT AT THE COUNTY LEVEL

ROBERT REYNOLDS, County of San Diego

Examples of community cooperation to reduce alcohol problems abound in our society. Unfortunately, most of these examples involve what Mark Worden has labeled popular prevention: efforts directed at involving functioning individuals in life enchancement activities (Worden, 1979:425). In the alcohol field there is a plethora of in-school programs that incorporate information giving, values clarification, and peer counseling, which usually enjoy broad-based community cooperation. In our prevention efforts in San Diego County we encourage speaker invitations to Soroptimist and Rotary luncheons, court favorable attention from the news media, and sponsor neighborhood coffee klatches and community forums. Most of these efforts are premised on the notion that if individuals had better information or felt better about themselves, then they would not develop alcohol problems. Despite the lack of any substantive evidence that these activities produce the desired result, we persist in these efforts because they are, indeed, popular.

Given the magnitude of our community alcohol problems, it is evident that individually focused prevention efforts, even if proven effective, are unacceptably inefficient. As a society we simply cannot afford to thoroughly educate every citizen about alcohol problems and the use of alcoholic beverages. Fortunately, we have an alternative—a choice

137

perhaps best exemplified by our responses to other community problems.

For example, when we have a dangerous traffic intersection we very seldom mount a campaign to educate the public about the dangers of the intersection. Instead, we install a traffic light or in serious instances we construct an overpass. In short, we alter the physical environment in lieu of attempting to modify individual behavior through increased awareness of the problem. This alternative response is both efficient and effective, but until recently similar response systems have seldom been employed in responding to community alcohol problems.

The National Research Council's report *Alcohol and Public Policy: Beyond the Shadow of Prohibition* provides focus to prevention policies that ". . . operate in a nonpersonal way to alter the set of contingencies affecting individuals as they drink or engage in activities that . . . are considered risky" (Moore and Gerstein, 1981:53). Regrettably, the alcoholism constituency has limited experience in generating community cooperation in support of policies designed to change the circumstances of the drinking event. Until recently, post-Prohibition prevention efforts had been largely directed at changing the drinker per se. In spite of this limited experience, we may expect tremendous expansion of community support during this decade of prevention efforts designed to reduce alcohol problems through direct alteration of the drinking environment.

Basis for Optimism

There are four main reasons for optimism. First, in the past decade there has been a dramatic increase in our society's acceptance and definition of alcohol problems. Alcohol problems are now a topic of community discussion at the local, state, and national level, and this discussion is no longer narrowly focused on the alcoholic. As a society we are beginning to recognize that drunk driver problems, stadium crowd control problems, home accidents and violence, and many other alcohol-related problems cannot be blamed exclusively on the alcoholic. As an example, a study recently completed in San Diego demonstrated that of those convicted for a first-time drunk driver offense, fewer than 20 percent exhibited serious drinking problems, compared with 80 percent of those with second convictions (Ryan and Segars, 1983). Thus, as our society redefines alcohol problems and the causes of these problems, our definition of prevention policies must also change.

Second, the groups and individuals historically involved in providing alcoholism services have begun to acknowledge resource limitations and the need for new allies. As the definition of alcohol problems expands, and as institutions across our nation confront the limitations of public- as well as private-sector resources, the historical alcoholism constituencies are forced to face the reality that there will always be insufficient resources to provide direct personal recovery services to all those in need. While prevention efforts have always received lip service, this acceptance of resource limitations has belatedly begun to generate a genuine interest in prevention policies focused on societal rather than individual changes.

Third, recent prevention policy research has presented new options for community cooperation in reducing alcohol problems. As recently as three years ago the literature was essentially devoid of discussion of the impacts of minimum age restrictions, media portrayal of alcohol consumption, beverage labeling, excise tax levels, bartender liability and training, and other similar policy issues. The emergence of this literature will provide guidance and encouragement to community efforts to reduce alcohol problems.

Finally, success tends to have a catalytic effect. Community groups are beginning to again become involved in efforts to reduce community alcohol problems. While the negative consequences of Prohibition have long been interpreted as demonstration that alcohol problems cannot be managed or resolved through controls on alcohol availability, local community experience is beginning to challenge this interpretation. As communities have confronted specific alcohol problems, they have rediscovered that these problems can be resolved and that controls on alcohol availability are an important factor in problem resolution. Whether directed at alcohol problems occurring at a public beach or park, a sports stadium, or a neighborhood corner, the availability of alcohol itself is increasingly acknowledged as a legitimate concern. While community prevention efforts have typically been focused on small-scale neighborhood problems, success in resolving these issues of limited scope has encouraged a community willingness to respond to alcohol problems of a broader scope.

Initiation of Prevention Efforts

Most frequently, we discuss and analyze prevention efforts that have been initiated through the efforts of individuals in the field of alcoholism. Special projects and campaigns understandably draw our attention and our praise or criticism. These efforts typically identify a problem, define its magnitude, initiate an awareness campaign, and hope that awareness will generate concern and then action. This hope is seldom realized, and the critics announce that another prevention effort has failed.

This failure is not difficult to understand. Prevention efforts that seek to make the special concerns of those in the field of alcoholism the concern of the general community must be extremely well designed and conducted to be successful. In short, it is very difficult to convince others that "my" problem should become "their" problem, and it is even more difficult to convince the community that this problem is of such priority as to merit individual time, money, or changed behavior.

While it is certainly understandable that the alcoholism constituency has concentrated on its self-initiated efforts, this parochialism has diverted attention and resources from other, more spontaneous, and probably more successful community prevention efforts. The alcohol problem most likely to motivate an individual or group to action is the problem that emerges from a personal crisis, e.g., a child killed by a drunk driver or a business suffering declining floor traffic due to street drinking. These events, and the resulting opportunities for mobilizing concern into action, are not predictable. Who can predict the death of a Carrie Lightner and the resultant development of Mothers Against Drunk Drivers? Who knows when central business district employers will join together in opposition to public inebriation, or when parents will object to student drinking at school social events? Ultimately, action initiated within the community is the action most likely to seize the community agenda and provide the opportunity for successful community cooperation to reduce alcohol problems.

Too often, however, these opportunities are lost. People are otherwise engaged, and bureaucracies are often insensitive to community initiatives. Consequently, initial community action is too frequently allowed to dissipate. All too seldom are those interested in prevention policies able to capture the public's attention; we in the alcohol field must learn to respond with sensitivity, support, and creativity to the opportunities provided by others.

Role of Prevention Staff

Community denial of alcohol problems is still pervasive in American society. For alcohol program staff who have worked to achieve recognition of these problems, the emerging community acknowledgment of alcohol problems can pose an ironic dilemma. While community denial of alcohol problems and the consequent lack of recognition of past accomplishment and effort have frustrated alcohol program staff, the emerging community acceptance of alcohol problems is in fact primarily predicated on responses to individual losses or problems identified as external to the alcohol constituency. While recognition of past efforts may well be deserved, such recognition does not advance community initiative to resolve alcohol problems.

Community members often become involved in community alcohol problems for intensely personal reasons. The personal motivation is usually quite immediate and may relate to a tragic event or loss. With such individuals the recounting of prior staff efforts to resolve the problem is likely to be discounted or rejected and is often resented because of prior perceived failures. In fact, unless staff can relate on a personal level to the problem identified, whether it be loss of business, property, family, health, or comfort, staff involvement in problem resolution is likely to require both explanation and justification.

Whether it is the common experience of concerned parents, aroused neighbors, or victims of drunk drivers, it is this common anger or frustration that provides the initial fuel for community cooperation to reduce alcohol problems. Staff experience, no matter how expert, must remain secondary and supportive. The challenge is to weave staff knowledge into the analysis of the problem without detracting from the sense that the group is capable of and responsible for resolving it.

Arenas for Action

Certain areas of recurring concern can be expected to provide fruitful arenas for prevention efforts, whether initiated by the alcoholism constituency or by the general community. While many classes of concerns are possible, Friedner Wittman (1982) has developed a helpful structure:

1. Problems of neighborhood tranquillity, including rowdy outlets, late-night drinking and parties, and drinking in public places.

2. Concerns about alcohol outlets, including sales to minors and the relationship of alcohol outlets to crime and vice.

3. Concerns about drinking and driving, including accidents, enforcement levels, and freeway-oriented outlets.

4. Young people's and minors' uses of alcohol, including problems of growth and maturation and social interactions.

5. Public inebriates and alcohol problem areas, including public and private-sector costs and inconveniences.

Clearly there are other areas of community concern about alcohol problems; however, problems in these five areas exist and surface from time to time in almost every American community. Those with an interest in resolving alcohol problems should prepare generalized strategies of response for each of these problem types, remain sensitive to emerging community concerns, and be able to tailor involvement and activities to each specific event generating community interest. Thus, prevention planning becomes less a matter of predesigned campaigns, slogans, and media events, and more a matter of contingency planning and support for community-initiated concerns and events that, while unscheduled, are predictable in their general theme.

A number of planned responses could be developed for each problem type. For instance, for concerns about alcohol outlets, community responses could include efforts to improve bartender training, to reduce hours of sale or occupancy limits, to increase police presence, and to improve physical settings such as noise barriers or parking lot lighting. When a specific community concern is identified, these options should be tailored for application to the presenting problem. Advance planning will help ensure that a full range of options is examined in the development of an integrated response, thus avoiding incomplete problem analysis, single-dimensional responses, and ultimately unsatisfactory problem resolution.

Principles for Success

There are at least six principles that when followed promote successful community cooperation to reduce alcohol problems. First, groups must listen to each other. To succeed, community coalitions established to reduce alcohol problems must draw support from a broad field of interests. The view of the problem and position of each coalition member will vary, but these divergent positions must be understood and accepted by the group as a whole if the coalition is to succeed.

As an example, the problem of street drinking and public inebriety might involve the following interests, problem definitions, and solutions:

Interest Group	Perceived Primary Problem	Perceived Primary Solution
Merchants	Loss of business	Eliminate street drinkers
Sheriff	Jail overcrowding	Expand jail
City police	Merchant complaints	Additional police officers
Courts	Crowded dockets	Reduce arrests/Add judges
Church missions	Indigents needing food and housing	Expansion of resources
Alcohol program	Alcoholics needing treatment	Additional treatment programs
Street drinkers	Police harassment	Jobs and housing
Shoppers/Employees	Panhandling/Safety fears	Eliminate street drinkers

Each group has a legitimate interest in the problem and a particular view of the problem and solution. However, it is only through open communication that these groups will be able to avoid conflict. Often the perceived solution for one group (additional police officers) contributes to the perceived problems (crowded court dockets, jail overcrowding) of another group equally committed to resolution of the initial problem (public inebriety).

Second, underlying assumptions must be challenged. Few areas are as fraught with myths as are alcohol problems. Typical examples include the common belief that most drunk drivers are alcoholics and that central-city street people are primarily public inebriates. In the example of public inebriety described above, each interest group has made certain assumptions about the nature of the problem and the solutions. After each group has an opportunity to be heard and understood, the assumptions of each must be challenged before they are accepted as a basis for action. This challenge often involves the next principle.

Third, problems must be precisely defined, described, and disaggregated. Social survey research is especially helpful in this effort. In San Diego it was discovered that individuals arrested by the police for public inebriety were not as transient (only 19 percent with under a year's residency, 56 percent with over 5 years' residency), as old (42 percent under 30, only 9 percent over 60), or as frequently a problem (88 percent picked up once per month, only 6 percent more often than twice per month) as commonly assumed (Wynne, 1982a, 1982b). These data were essential in defining central-city problems and designing achievable and successful responses to them.

Fourth, responsibility for each problem segment must be both identified and defined. Often responsibility is jointly held, but mutual responsibility must be acknowledged and accepted by the responsible parties before cooperative effort can begin. At times it is difficult for groups to acknowledge mutual responsibility. In fact, many prevention efforts are initiated by one group accusing another of failing in its responsibilities. Merchants often blame street drinking problems on lack of police action, while failing to recognize that the police do not distribute and sell alcoholic beverages. Placing blame is counterproductive and must be replaced with acceptance of mutual responsibility if a successful coalition is to be sustained.

Fifth, all involved parties must move forward in an integrated and incremental response to the problem. Independent and sudden or dramatic actions should be avoided to decrease the likelihood of unintended negative consequences for other coalition members. Clearly, unilateral and unexpected increased police actions in a central-city area can overwhelm community jail, court, health, and social service systems. Changes in agency procedures or policies should be carefully coordinated to avoid negative impacts on others. In addition, such sudden and uncoordinated changes pose unnecessary risks. Communities and community alcohol problems are dynamic. Few alcohol problems can be resolved by a single action. Most actions create a reaction and probably a new problem. Even with the best planning, these new problems are difficult to predict. Incremental implementation of new policies and procedures provides for a margin of error and an opportunity for assessment. This permits midcourse corrections to minimize the development of serious new problems.

The five principles presented above are dynamic and nonlinear. They are most effective when applied simultaneously and continuously, which is the sixth principle. While listening must never stop, discussion and consensus must not become goals in and of themselves. Assumptions must be challenged, problems defined, responsible parties identified, and action plans implemented. Community prevention efforts are beginning. However, there is no middle or end to these efforts. Although alcohol problems may change or their magnitude increase or decrease, they are very seldom eliminated. Even as one prevention plan is implemented, new problems emerge in a complex drinking society, with new underlying assumptions, providing additional challenges and opportunities.

Prospects

In this era community cooperation to reduce alcohol problems is still a relatively rare phenomenon. Our society is only beginning to cease blaming the individual alcoholic for the full range of alcohol problems in society. As we begin to overcome our collective denial of societal alcohol problems, there are signs that we are beginning to accept our collective responsibility for them.

As helpful as prevention grants and staff experts may be, our hope rests primarily with the reemergence of citizen-initiated prevention efforts. Beginning on a small scale, community groups are discovering that alcohol problems can be moderated. Community cooperation to reduce alcohol problems is synergistic. This emerging cooperation promises to become the catalyst for affecting the societal changes necessary to reduce alcohol problems. This new social movement may well lead to major redefinitions of the role of alcohol in our society in the years ahead.

REGULATION AND EDUCATION IN A UNIVERSITY COMMUNITY

DAVID P. KRAFT, University of Massachusetts, Amherst

The Demonstration Alcohol Education Project at the University of Massachusetts, Amherst

The University of Massachusetts at Amherst is the main undergraduate and graduate campus of the state university. The enrollment is approximately 22,000 students, over half of whom live in university housing. During the decade between 1973 and 1983, the campus focused special attention on alcohol-related problems. With the assistance of a federally funded grant from the National Institute on Alcohol Abuse and Alcoholism (NIAAA) for approximately $600,000 between 1975 and 1980, the campus attempted to study ways of influencing communitywide practices to reduce alcohol problems. The program developed certain methods that combined educational and regulatory approaches in a consistent fashion and became a "model" used by other university campuses. Extensive evaluation of program efforts produced a mixture of results that may be useful to prevention efforts in many locations (Duston et al., 1981; Kraft, in press). Campus efforts since 1980 have capitalized on these findings.

The Demonstration Alcohol Education Project (DAEP) at the University of Massachusetts relied heavily on community development principles with various campus constituencies. The program combined awareness-raising mass media approaches, small group educational efforts and community-supported special efforts, and behavioral regulations to effect changes. Program planning and evaluation tasks were guided by the PRECEDE health education model developed by Green and associates (1980). PRECEDE requires that specific adverse health consequences be defined and then analyzed to determine factors in the individual as well as the environment that inhibit or facilitate antecedent health-related behaviors. The model helped identify specific factors that needed to be addressed not only in individual students, but also in affiliative groups of students, key leaders of the institution and campus groups, drinking settings, and treatment resources. The PRECEDE model is consistent with the Fishbein and Ajzen (1975) theory of behavior change, which suggests that a person's intention to change his or her behavior can be influenced not only by knowledge, attitude, and belief changes in the individual but also by changes in community norms.

The Problems

The perceived problems on campus shifted over time. For example, in 1973-1974, campus leaders were concerned about the number of "alcoholics" that seemed to be increasing and was especially reflected in alcohol-related dorm damage and arrests. Subsequent research actually showed that alcohol consumption had remained unchanged between 1971 and 1974, according to random surveys, and no more than 20 alcoholics (0.1 percent of the student population) could be identified through a review of comprehensive health records. However, the abuse of illicit drugs had certainly decreased between 1971 and 1974, and many periodic drinkers other than alcoholics were found to have experienced alcohol problems. Beginning in 1975, campus leaders focused most of their attention on alcohol-related problems, including health problems, dorm damage related to parties, and campus police arrests in the following four categories: driving under the influence (DUI); protective custody (PC); malicious destruction and vandalism (MD&V); and disturbing the peace (DP). DAEP attempted to influence these behaviors. By 1979, after the legal drinking age had been raised from 18 to 20, concerns focused more heavily on minor accidental injuries, emotional problems, underage drinking on and off campus, and increased arrests for DWI and PC. (While dorm damage actually increased, DAEP studies had shown that much of it was not directly attributable to alcohol use.) By 1982, attention had shifted more directly to students with arrests for DWI and with disciplinary problems related to alcohol use.

The historical shifts reported above reflected careful work that regularly attempted to define the kinds and extent of alcohol problems that prevailed on campus. Very quickly, key community members began to realize that the highest proportion of alcohol problems occurred among both regular and occasional heavy consumers of alcohol, only some of whom would be defined as "alcoholic" by any standard criteria. The focus of community alcohol program efforts rapidly shifted to preventing certain problems by a variety of strategies, only some of which focused on heavy drinkers, including alcoholics.

Over the 5 years of DAEP, specific alcohol problems were recorded by both self-report surveys and community agencies. Each year a significant proportion of students reported driving under the influence (an average of 29 percent), academic problems (23 percent), minor physical injuries (17 percent), abusive behavior (16 percent), and job-related difficulties (14 percent) related to drinking. Property damage (7 percent) and alcohol dependence (1 percent) were also reported by a smaller proportion of students (Kraft, in press).

Many of the adverse drinking-related behaviors seemed to be associated with social events, including campus parties and drinking at pubs and bars. Survey data revealed that heavier-drinking students frequently attended both parties and pubs or bars (Kraft, 1981) and were more likely to experience adverse consequences than lighter or moderate drinkers. During the survey, which followed the raising of the legal drinking age from 18 to 20, the proportion of students reporting driving under the influence increased from 32 percent in October 1978 to 42 percent in October 1979 (Kraft, in press).

Campus and Town Involvement

The campus community was involved in DAEP activities and was monitored in an ongoing fashion. The relationship between campus perceptions and programmatic response was dynamic and evolutionary. For example, in 1973 the perceived problems of "alcoholics" led to an Alcohol Task Force in 1974-1975 that involved staff of the health services, police, dormitories, and the office of the dean of students. The result was a more general focus on drinking problems and the pursuit of federal funding for a campus alcohol abuse prevention project. In 1975, the receipt of federal funding led to an extensive effort to prevent alcohol problems by the use of peer education methods, mass media and public education efforts, intensive educational workshops for students, and active involvement of community groups and agencies.

By 1977, problems related to campus parties (e.g., dorm damage, personal injuries, and questions of staff liability for party injuries) led to the establishment of an Alcohol Beverage Policy Task Force, composed of an equal number of the staff and students most concerned. The result was the implementation in September 1978 of a comprehensive party-planning policy that defined the responsibilities and training required for party planners, bartenders, security personnel, and staff supervisors for medium- and large-size parties.

The policy showed initial positive effects until April 1979, when the legal drinking age was raised from 18 to 20, making it illegal for most on-campus students to drink. Another task force was convened that revised party-planning regulations to retain most of the important features of the previous policy. More significantly, reduced revenues at the on-campus pub led to cooperative efforts between the pub managers and DAEP staff to produce an attractive social center for students of all ages. We struggled with ways to improve the supply picture, such as changing practices so that the pubs would make as much profit on a pitcher of Coke for underage students as they used to make on a pitcher of beer.

In 1981, a fatal accident in Amherst involving four youths who had been drinking mobilized constructive "town-gown" cooperation to begin the Safety Action Program. It included both education about drinking and driving in the secondary schools and on college campuses, and stricter, highly visible enforcement of drunk driving laws with subsequent convictions. Finally, in 1982, questions by off-campus bar owners regarding liability for accidents caused by drunken patrons leaving and attempting to drive led to an expansion of the campus bartender training to off-campus establishments. In the same year on-campus disciplinary cases, mainly involving alcohol-related abusive behavior and property damage, led to a special group education effort called the Student Opportunity Program. Students were helped to control their behavior before they experienced more severe disciplinary actions, including suspension.

Most of the changes made over the decade between 1973 and 1983 had been identified in the preliminary needs assessments made in 1973 and 1974. However, the needs often could not be adequately addressed until relevant individuals or groups in the community became sufficiently concerned to help effect necessary changes. Also, many of the resultant changes might not have occurred if alcohol program personnel had not been alert and available to guide naturally occurring interests and events in a constructive direction (e.g., the 1977 conflict between students and staff over dormitory parties and the 1981 highway fatalities, which initially threatened to place the town and the university against each other).

Five general steps were developed based on the prevention experience at the university:

1. Determine the problems related to alcohol that concern community members most. Common themes and independently validated perceptions are important to pursue. List specific problems, not general categories of "drinkers," as much as possible.

2. Enlist aid in developing and continuing the programs, not only from those personally interested in the topic under discussion but also those agencies and/or key leaders who can influence or implement changes that might be needed. Involvement of key individuals and groups usually requires the recognition and use of each person's self-interests in the issues at hand.

3. Using the list of problems developed above, examine the evidence regarding the actual as well as the perceived extent of each problem and the factors that may contribute. Avoid either jumping to premature and oversimplified solutions until sufficient data have been examined or refusing to act once sufficient clarity has developed, even though the data are not conclusive or exhaustive.

4. Engage as many of the interested and necessary groups as possible in a cooperative endeavor to design the solutions, especially if they will have to implement or enforce certain changes or will be the target of certain actions. In cases in which self-interest may impede progress, graduated steps may help overcome initial resistance. For example, if a voluntary educational approach is not effective to correct a certain problem within a specified period of time, then a more direct approach may need to be employed.

5. Evaluate the results in an ongoing manner and refine strategies accordingly. Use a combination of systematic observations, special surveys of "gatekeepers," and random surveys of individuals. The evaluation method should not be fancier than the accuracy of the data to be analyzed. Any change in a community system will also create or uncover new problems that require further study and evaluation.

The Results of Community-Based Efforts

Between 1975 and 1980, DAEP efforts focused on specific problems, especially party-related behaviors, driving under the influence, disrupted personal relationships, and interrupted personal career goals. Extensive approaches raised the awareness of up to 70 percent of students on campus about important alcohol messages through the use of posters, newspaper advertisements and articles, radio advertisements and interviews, and special displays in the student center (Kelly, 1978). Intensive, face-to-face educational efforts were used to reach about 10 percent of students each year. Most involved single-session, small group discussions led by peer educators (i.e., trained students) and were held in dormitories or apartments. Close to 0.5 percent of students participated in multiple-session group discussions or academic courses on prevention each year. Community development efforts concentrated on key groups, agencies, and leaders according to the perceived needs and interests of both program staff and targeted personnel or groups. One result was that about 5 percent of staff and faculty of the university were involved in staff training each year, especially staff in the residence halls. Another result was involvement in an ongoing sequence of special groups to study and modify various regulatory practices both at the university level (e.g., party-planning guidelines) and at the individual agency level (e.g., bartender training at the on-campus pub).

Efforts were evaluated in a number of ways. The most "scientific" evaluation instrument was a self-report questionnaire sent to a random sample of between 1,200 and 1,450 students each year with a response rate of between 60 and 70 percent. Special surveys were also conducted with intermediate-level observers, including dormitory heads, medical staff, mental health staff, and campus police. Indirect "archival" data were examined for any trends, including routine reports reflecting dormitory damage, alcohol-related arrests, alcohol-related medical and mental health visits, and party permits. Finally, special controlled studies of specific educational attempts were conducted to determine the relative value or effects of such efforts to change attitudes and behaviors (Kraft, in press).

At the individual level most students learned certain facts and agreed with desired attitudes about alcohol. Program efforts also attracted the attention of a slightly higher proportion of the "at risk" population than other students, namely heavier drinkers, younger students, and students living on campus. However, no significant decrease in drinking behaviors or adverse consequences were noted among a random sample of students during DAEP. The only significant decreases in problem drinking behaviors were noted in students who participated in multiple-session educational programs designed to train them to teach other students.

At the intermediate-observer level, a number of changes occurred. In the dormitories, a significant increase was observed over the five years in the number of parties that included nonalcoholic food and beverages, and in the active confrontation of problem drinkers by other students in an attempt to change their behaviors, including referrals to treatment resources. Among helping agencies, more staff reported recognizing alcohol problems much earlier and attempting to make appropriate interventions.

Archival data proved useless in measuring the actual occurrence of alcohol problems. Most episodes measured are either low-frequency events (e.g., DUI arrests compared with the actual proportion of students reporting driving under the influence) or are so inaccurate due to a variety of other factors that no confidence could be placed in them (Kraft, in press).

Special studies did show important results. One-session group discussions did not result in behavioral changes whereas multiple-session discussion groups did show such changes. Media efforts can produce changes in knowledge about simple facts, such as the equivalent alcohol content of beer, wine, and liquor, without leading to behavior changes. Other studies also confirmed that significant changes did occur at aggregate levels, such as observations about party planning behavior, without being reflected in self-reported individual patterns of drinking.

Finally, special spot surveys conducted on a regular basis with medical and mental health staff confirmed much higher levels of people seen with alcohol problems than indicated on routine archival reports.

Since the conclusion of DAEP, alcohol education efforts have continued with a reduced level of specific alcohol-program personnel. Various facets have been integrated within the ongoing efforts of other involved groups, such as party planning and early problem detection activities of residence hall staff, and bartender training and supervision by campus pub managers.

Conclusions

Community involvement in the prevention of alcohol problems in a college population is extremely important. Efforts to enlist and utilize community resources at the University of Massachusetts at Amherst over the past decade have demonstrated these main points:

1. *Time Required*: Broad changes usually require a long time to develop (years and even decades), frequently in response to a series of unexpected needs and circumstances. The shape of program efforts shifts according to the self-interests and needs of individuals and groups involved.

2. *Specific Needs*: Cooperation usually develops in response to some combination of perceived and actual needs of community members to combat alcohol problems. Perceived needs are often based on myths or incomplete data. As much as possible, specific alcohol problems should be defined and assessed to determine the actual extent of a given problem, with solutions developed accordingly.

3. *Broad Strategies*: Solutions to alcohol-related problems should focus not only on directly modifying the drinking behaviors of individuals, but also on training friends and family as well as gatekeepers (bartenders, police, medical personnel, etc.), altering environmental factors (drinking environment, public transportation to and from bars, etc.), and establishing norms and regulations that are both reasonable and enforceable.

4. *Combined Approaches*: Methods of changing drinking behaviors should combine mass media approaches to focus attention and mobilize support with in-depth education of significant groups and individuals regarding the prevention of specific alcohol problems and enforcement of reasonable regulations. The combination of efforts can often change aggregate behaviors in significant ways without necessarily altering self-reported alcohol consumption levels of individuals. (Young people may drink the same amounts of alcohol, on average, but in safer ways.)

5. *Empowering Groups:* Cooperative efforts should continually seek to use diverse groups in the community to design and implement various strategies. The cooperative endeavors can give the various groups a common understanding and also a collective response to such problems as driving under the influence or underage drinking in schools.

6. *Treatment Sources*: Prevention efforts must be built on adequate treatment resources for people with drinking problems. The resources must not be limited to those needed for severe alcoholics but should include general counseling and health services for the broad spectrum of people with alcohol problems.

7. *Evaluation*: Efforts to evaluate programs must be built into each endeavor. The evaluation methods used need not be highly advanced or complicated, but should be systematic and honest in order to detect changes or effects, if any. Without such evaluation, resources may be inappropriately used, only to fade away when their ineffectiveness is finally discovered. Systematic evaluation can also help ensure ongoing community funding and support even if efforts are only moderately successful.

Community-based approaches seem to work best when they include a combination of education and regulation (or enforcement). Education alone, while ideally the most effective solution, is impractical. The amount of time and expense involved in attempting to modify unhealthy drinking beliefs and practices—not merely informing people of undesirable consequences—would take resources and cooperation well beyond most communities' financial base and certainly beyond their authority. Yet a small but significant group of educated citizens can influence constructive changes in community norms and practices that can lead to desired changes.

Regulation alone also can be fraught with difficulties of polarizing community residents with eventual rebellion in one form or another (often lax enforcement of an unpopular or unfair statute or law). Too often, regulations are developed and implemented with little input from various community constituencies and poor information disseminated to all residents concerning the need for regulations. The educational process can often make certain regulatory approaches more palatable and enforceable.

Community strategies should not focus solely on changing alcohol consumption but also on changing people's reactions to a given behavior (e.g., a bar owner not allowing a drunken patron to drive home) or insulating problem behaviors from undesirable consequences (e.g., providing free bus service between popular drinking establishments and major living areas or encouraging drunken guests to sleep overnight).

In fact, efforts to involve the "alcohol distribution centers" (i.e., bars, restaurants, off-premise stores) with public information, trained personnel, and modified practices are frequently ignored in community-based programs. Due to fears of liability, many establishments are now eager for useful training and assistance in some communities.

Although difficult to achieve and maintain, community-level strategies can influence drinking behaviors more effectively than approaches based solely on individual education approaches. In fact, a combination of education and regulation proved to be the most effective way to produce community-level changes at the University of Massachusetts.

COMMENTS ON COMMUNITY COOPERATION AND KNOWLEDGE DISSEMINATION

FRIEDNER WITTMAN, Medical Research Institute of San Francisco

James Mosher, Lawrence Wallack, and I have developed a Community Substance Abuse Assistance Program in the San Francisco Bay area for the kind of community organizing that Mr. Reynolds talked about. Our emphasis has been to draw together representatives of each of the major sectors in the community. We held a series of workshops last year in San Francisco, attended by about 20 people representing the Public Defenders' Office, the City Planning Department, the downtown development area of San Francisco, the alcoholism treatment services community, the mayor's office, the Board of Supervisors, the local office of the Alcoholic Beverage Control Department, Wine Institute, etc. By pulling together these major actors, we developed a community of concern to begin sharing values and approaches to dealing with alcohol problems. We can report that organizing such a community group takes quite a lot of energy and a very heavy commitment of time. Just calling the first meeting was a major difficulty. But once we pulled together people from these constituencies, the ball began to roll and synergistic things began to happen.

A critical incident was an oil company petition to the city to permit mixing alcoholic beverage and gasoline sales in drive-through mini-mart operations. That served as a galvanizing or rallying point around which the different people in the group could contribute their skills, resulting in the withdrawal of the petition to change the city ordinance. This success occurred while we were in the midst of calling together, planning, and organizing these meetings. It is a small example of how calling people together and identifying areas of shared concern can work.

We recommend working with the highest level of people in charge of agencies, institutions, and organizations as well as at the grass-roots level of neighborhoods. Moving back and forth between these two levels, we think, is most effective.

CATHERINE ANDERSON, Metropolitan Pittsburgh Public Broadcasting

I would like to note how a major outreach campaign began in public broadcasting to fight teenage drug and alcohol abuse. In May 1981, WQED-TV in Pittsburgh launched a major campaign in western Pennsylvania. We developed 12 hours of programming and created a task force composed of elected officials, the police, the universities, the churches, and so forth. Each of the people on the task force took responsibility for local high school communities and formed local task forces. Those task forces, we were told, would dry up over the summer. But by the fall, we had 112—now 114. So we decided to make this a national outreach project called "Chemical People." We received grants from the Metropolitan Life Foundation and from the Mellon Foundation to do this. The White House is involved; Nancy Reagan hosted 2 hours of prime-time programming on public television. We have gotten 26 national organizations, including the National Council on Alcoholism, the National Council of Churches, PTAs, Junior Leagues, Kiwanis, Lions, and similar kinds of groups involved and committed to work on this project. Our goal is to create task forces in every high school community in this country. Public television stations have agreed to carry these national programs; most of them also agreed to produce a local program to talk about their particular problem and to spearhead the task force outreach in their community.

ROBERT ROSS, State of New York

I recently attended a meeting of the Planning Group of Southeast Bronx. That community was so devastated in 1967-1968 that they are almost rebuilding the entire area; the planning group has an enormous amount of control over what gets back into the community. It is an interesting and rather eclectic group, consisting of religious and local business leaders, people who live or work in the community, etc. They represent not only people interested in social issues but also people interested from an economic point of view. As an example of the kind of policy issues that they focus on, the group has taken a very strong stand on housing and has prevented the building of any new high-rise residential buildings.

I made an informal presentation on alcohol issues related to youth, and one of the questions after the meeting was whether we could provide any guidance that could prevent the density of liquor outlets, both bars and package stores that had been there before, from returning to that community. The business leaders there were saying, "We only want certain kinds of businesses coming back." They are looking for guidance; state alcohol agencies, in providing information and direction for local guidance, can be very helpful. This community group does not want to see the problems replicated, and they want to feel that they can have some control over it. One of the things that our state agency focuses on is acquiring a better understanding of natural support groups that are tangential to the alcoholism provider network but would have a lot of impact—in some cases more than the alcoholism service providers—in determining local policy.

HENRY KING, United States Brewers Association

The range of local options varies with different state constitutions. For instance, in North Carolina a community can vote wet or dry. If they vote dry, they have no outlets. If they vote wet, they are allowed to have so many per population. Each state has different alcoholic beverage laws. We are talking about 230 million people living in a country in which there are established patterns of sales and distribution. So I do not think availability per se is the issue as much as the manner in which alcohol is made available. If the goal is to reduce consumption by reducing the number of outlets, there is just no way you can do that successfully with what is in place now. As a practical matter, it is not a reasonable option for those who want to reduce consumption.

ROBERT REYNOLDS, County of San Diego

But specific disaggregated alcohol problems are susceptible to change at the local level. There are many strategies that are the prerogatives of local government, such as zoning, that can be used in heavily impacted areas. Why should a community not choose to refuse more outlets if, for example, its alcohol-related crime rate is already 20 percent above the norm? Communities can mobilize around those kinds of issues and have an impact on the number of outlets permitted. In our central-city redevelopment in San Diego, the community testified against a certain type of drinking—street drinking. A poor black community organized around the ready accessibility of package sales, because they did their drinking at home; you could not go anywhere in that community without seeing ready access to alcoholic beverages. In a skid row area, too, I think the community has a right and an obligation to reduce outlets and consumption.

Let me cite a different example of land use that is subject to local control: stadium sales. Is there any real reason to continue the sale of beer and wine in a stadium after the seventh inning, when people are about to drive out? Or in recreation sites: in many of our parks, distilled beverages are not permitted but beer and wine are, and we are steadily increasing our police force there. These are areas of availability that do not specifically have to do with licensing regulations, but with local values and mores.

PHILIP COOK, Duke University

Do you think, to take the example of reducing the number of outlets in a community, that if someone has to walk an extra block, or three or four extra blocks for a drink, that would make a difference for the neighborhood?

ROBERT REYNOLDS, County of San Diego

I think spontaneous buying is a very important factor, but we have a paucity of evidence demonstrating this relationship. We have very little social research, prevention research. Sociocultural and environmental research proposals go to grant review panels of psychological and biological researchers, which give them very low priority. Typically, we are still looking for the pill, the biological factor. We still cling to the old notion that alcoholics cause all these problems. We are only beginning to understand that alcoholics contribute only part of the alcohol problems of our society. The number of cross-cultural and demographic studies in the area of alcohol abuse in our society is pitifully small.

When you try to focus a specific intervention, when you look at a specific type of problem, you often do not have the data to apply to that specific instance. DWI is a good example. Who are the DWI drivers? They are impaired, and we too often confuse drunkenness with impairment. In my county, they tend to be young, white male adults who—if you look at the Cahalan studies of drinking in the general population (Cahalan et al., 1969)—are getting drunk on weekends in the manner characteristic of that age stratum. Relatively few—in our studies less than 20 percent—have addictive drinking problems. Without these kind of data you do not really know how to intervene. I am persuaded by the basic formula of increased availability leading to increased consumption leading to increased problems. But when we try to intervene with a specific problem, this kind of collective data falls apart. The proposition needs to be studied in a variety of settings and levels, making use of detailed demographic and survey research data.

MICHAEL GOODSTADT, Alcoholism and Drug Addiction Research Foundation

But would the data that do exist suggest that we should become more liberal? This is similar to the debate on television violence. For a long time people said that it is not proven that violence portrayed on television causes violence in society. But the data at that time, in the 1960s and the early 1970s, at least would have led you to be conservative, not to increase the amount of violence. In the case of alcohol, quite a number of studies, in addition to common sense, would suggest that we should stop making alcohol ever more available in the many ways it becomes more available—increased per capita number of outlets, letting the price drop as the cost of living increases, lowering the drinking age, making it permissible to drink in places other than licensed premises or at home (camping sites and so forth)—all these "liberalization" measures. The data are not sterling, you would not stake your entire reputation on any single study, but collectively you would say, "Hold on." If we are going to make a change—and there are pressures for change from all of us, in all parts of Western society—then at least we should attempt to assess it, always to ask ahead of time what are the likely implications of this proposed change for health and other aspects of things based on common sense and the data. We should look, as far as we can, at the impact, and try to act sensibly in light of what we can anticipate.

MICHAEL FOX, Ohio General Assembly

Another area in which we need more information is cataloging costs and evaluating programs. As we fight for dollars and compete for scarce resources across the board in the budgeting process at the state and local levels, the pressure to determine which social programs are cost-effective will increase. As a legislator and as a policy maker, one of the most frustrating things I deal with is the number of great plans—"Let's do this in the courts, let's do this in the schools." (I have my own drug education package that I am trying to get into the schools, but most of the superintendents I talk to tell me that we could spend $100 million and not have an impact on the problem.) A resource that pulls together the social costs in the criminal justice system, the health care system, the drunk driving fatalities, the teenage population problems—that catalogs these costs and offers a menu from which we can choose programs that have proven to be successful in a cost-effective way—would be extremely useful to policy makers, in the legislatures and state bureaucracies, and in county governments.

MARILYN GOLDWATER, Maryland House of Delegates

Does some mechanism exist to pull together this kind of data and disseminate this information? It seems to me that there are many different things going on, and it is important not only to evaluate them but also to disseminate the information around the country so that others can try them. The federal government works very well in disseminating information to counterparts in the state bureaucracy, for example, but not as well in getting information to state legislators, who also make policy.

FRANK PADAVAN, New York State Senate

The federal government could be very helpful if it would make such a resource available. For example, we have heard about liability for serving underage minors who later get involved in an auto accident. A number of states have it; a number of legislators in other states would like to have it. How effective is it and what are its positive benefits? It would be helpful to get that information to the state legislatures.

When we were considering raising the drinking age in New York (which we did in 1982), we were not able to draw on an easily usable body of knowledge. I had to assign a researcher, and it took a lot of time and effort. We did pull it all together; we did present the case; we did publish a report, as did the state executive department. That was a lot of effort to expend. I hope that in the aftermath of this conference someone could make available to us information about things that have worked effectively that we are interested in accomplishing on our individual turfs, such as civil liability. It is a question of getting all the relevant data and analysis together, evaluating it, making it concise— we do not really have the resources to do that, as much as we would like to.

DONALD McCONNELL, State of Connecticut

A body of knowledge about model programs has been created. The old Law Enforcement Assistance Administration (LEAA) of the U.S.

Department of Justice had model programs in criminal justice that could be replicated. That knowledge still exists somewhere, even though LEAA has been reorganized. The National Institute on Alcohol Abuse and Alcoholism has a national clearinghouse full of information relevant to programs and the evaluation of programs. The National Institute on Drug Abuse has a clearinghouse on programs that they have developed over the years. Some libraries have also put this material together; Rutgers has a fine library on the alcohol field, nationally and internationally. A lot of material has been collected and evaluated.

But we are generally weak on outcome indicators and longitudinal studies. During the years it takes to really evaluate a program, the scene changes, and the emphasis in society changes. Governments become interested in something else: holes in the highways rather than holes in the society.

FRANK RAFLO, County of Loudoun, Virginia

As for cataloging costs, one cost that is certainly rising faster than anything else is the cost of health, including and maybe especially mental health. I think that cost is being exacerbated considerably because of alcohol. For example, the social services board on which I serve has jurisdiction over one youngster who had an alcohol problem. He has been in a mental retardation rehabilitation center for 4 years, at a tuition of $28,000 a year. That is over $100,000 for one youngster—so far.

FRANK PADAVAN, New York State Senate

Mr. Raflo's point is buttressed by dollars-and-cents figures in New York. The cost of health care relevant to alcohol, directly or indirectly, has gone beyond the reach of any average individual, with large secondary and tertiary effects on the family, on the community, and on the employer. We are attempting in New York to mandate insurance carriers to provide alcoholism treatment in all group insurance plans to spread that burden.

MARK MOORE, Harvard University

With regard to the medical cost of chronic, intensive alcohol users: Researchers at Harvard Medical School studied high-cost medical care consumers. They turned out to be heavy smokers and drinkers, people who got sick early in life but not sick enough to die. They absorbed an enormous amount of the budget, far more than their proportion.

GAIL BURTON ALLEN, St. Luke's-Roosevelt Hospital Center

I direct an alcoholism treatment program in New York. People in the field estimate that 25-50 percent of the cases in general hospital services would, if diagnosed, carry a secondary diagnosis of alcoholism or alcohol abuse. This is a very significant fraction of medical costs. Cirrhosis is immediate, visible, and clearly measurable, but you must add general gastrointestinal diseases and all of the mental health problems. There is also the relation to child abuse, the delinquency of children of alcoholics, and the fact that these children are a high-risk population for general drug abuse and alcoholism. The costs are far-reaching and a little frightening.

LORAN ARCHER, National Institute on Alcohol Abuse and Alcoholism

A number of studies on the costs of alcoholism in terms of mental and physical health care have shown them to be quite substantial. As with the study of any disease, there are limitations to the knowledge we have. We are limited quite often to studies of admissions and therefore limited to how accurate the admission diagnosis is. We have been trying to refine and gather better information. People who manage those records need to be able to highlight the issue of cause and effect. It is like the question, "How many deaths are caused by smoking?" Very seldom does smoking per se show up as a cause of death or illness, so the numbers have to be inferred on the basis of epidemiological and clinical research. We have the same problem with alcohol.

We also need to build into the equation answers to the difficult question: What are the benefits of low-level alcohol use? We have started research from an epidemiological standpoint to look fairly at benefits and costs and balance the result. We have begun to show a substantial finding, as limited as the records are, in emergency room admissions, specific hospitals, and among high utilizers of health care. As gross as the figures are, we know that the cost is substantial. Alcohol has a tremendous impact on the health care system.

The NIAAA and the National Institute on Drug Abuse are working jointly with the states to develop a dissemination network for epidemiological data. We have a great deal of data. At the present time we can provide, down to the county level, a great deal of information on specific indicators such as traffic fatalities, cirrhosis, and other vital statistics. Our major problem is how to get the information disseminated, how to make that information available to state and local policy makers in a useful and easily accessible manner.

MARILYN GOLDWATER, Maryland House of Delegates

I think it is clear that a body of knowledge exists, and a more effective mechanism to gather all that knowledge and disseminate it to policy makers and other individuals who need it should be developed. The climate is now right, and we ought to take advantage of it. While I think we need still more research, we cannot wait for that research. I think that is why it is important to catalog now what is out there and disseminate it to policy makers.

References

Atkin, C., and Block, M.
1980   *Content and Effects of Alcohol Advertising. Report 1: Overview and Summary of the Project*. East Lansing, Mich.: Michigan State University.

Bandura, A.
1977   *Social Learning Theory*. Englewood Cliffs, N.J.: Prentice-Hall.

Beauchamp, D.
1976   Public health as social justice. *Inquiry* 12:3-14.
1980   *Beyond Alcoholism: Alcohol and Public Health Policy*. Philadelphia: Temple University Press.

Bonnie, R.
1981   Discouraging the use of alcohol, tobacco and other drugs: The effects of legal controls and restrictions. In N. Mello, *Advances in Substance Abuse Behavioral and Biological Research*. Vol. 2. New Haven, Conn.: JAI Press.

Bottom Line
1978   Taking another look at liquor advertising. *Bottom Line* 2(Fall):2-12.
1981   Beer advertising. *Bottom Line* 4(2):5.

Botvin, G., Eng., A., and Williams, C.
1980   Preventing the onset of cigarette smoking through life skills training. *Preventive Medicine* 9:135-143.

Breed, W., and DeFoe, J.
1979   Themes in magazine alcohol advertisements: A critique. *Journal of Drug Issues* 8:339-353.
1981   The portrayal of the drinking process on prime-time television. *Journal of Communication* 31(1):58-67.
1982   Effecting media change: The role of cooperative consultation on alcohol topics. *Journal of Communication* 32:100-111.

162

Bry, B.H.
1982 Reducing the incidence of adolescent problems through prevention intervention: one- and five-year follow-up. *American Journal of Community Psychology* 10:265-276.

Bry, B.H., and George, F.E.
1980 The preventive effects of early intervention upon the attendance and grades of urban adolescents. *Professional Psychology* 11:252-260.

Business Week
1981 What Edgar Bronfman wants at Seagram. *Business Week* April 27.
1982 Creating a mass market for wine. *Business Week* March 15:108-118.

Cahalan, D., Cisin, I.H., and Crossley, H.M.
1969 American Drinking Practices: A National Study of Drinking Behavior and Attitudes. Monograph no. 6. New Brunswick, N.J.: Rutgers Center of Alcohol Studies.

Calfiso, J., Goodstadt, M., Garlington, W., and Sheppard, M.
1982 Television protrayal of alcohol and other beverages. *Journal of Studies on Alcohol* 43(11):1232-1243.

Clark, W., and Midanik, L.
1981 *Alcohol Use and Alcohol Problems Among U.S. Adults: Results of the 1979 National Survey.* Berkeley, Calif.: Social Research Group.

Cohen, R.
1983 Miller time. Associated Press syndicated column. Thursday, February 10.

Comstock, G.
1976 Television and Alcohol Consumption and Abuse. Paper prepared at the request of Senator William B. Hathaway, Subcommittee on Alcoholism and Narcotics, U.S. Senate.

Cook, P.J.
1981 The effect of liquor taxes on drinking, cirrhosis, and auto accidents. Pp. 255-285 in M.H. Moore and D. Gerstein, eds., *Alcohol and Public Policy: Beyond the Shadow of Prohibition.* Washington, D.C.: National Academy Press.

Cook, P.J., and Tauchen, G.
1982 The effect of liquor taxes on heavy drinking. *Bell Journal of Economics* 13:379-390.

Council on Alcohol Policy Quarterly Newsletter
1983 New wine packaging, "refreshment beverages," and light wines—Key factors in projected 100% increase in consumption. *Council on Alcohol Policy Quarterly Newsletter* 2(1):7.

Dhalla, N.K.
1978 Assessing the long-term value of advertising. *Harvard Business Review* (Jan.-Feb.):87-95.

Dillin, J.
1975a TV drinking: How networks pour liquor into your living room. *Christian Science Monitor* 67(151):1ff.
1975b Can U.S. tune out TV drinking? *Christian Science Monitor* 67(152):1ff.
1975c TV drinking does not mirror U.S. *Christian Science Monitor* 67(162):4.

Duston, E.K., Kraft, D.P., and Jaworski, B.
1981 Alcohol education project: Preliminary answers. *Journal of the American College Health Association* 29:272-278.

Evans, R.I., Henderson, A.H., Hill, P., and Raines, B.E.
1979 Smoking in children and adolescents: Psychosocial determinants and prevention strategies. In *Smoking and Health: Report of the Surgeon General*. Available from the U.S. Superintendent of Documents, U.S. Government Printing Office, Washington, D.C.

Finn, T.A., and Strickland, D.E.
1982 A content analysis of beverage alcohol advertising: Television advertising. *Journal of Studies on Alcohol* 43(9):964-989.

Fishbein, M., and Ajzen, I.
1975 *Belief, Attitudes, Intention, and Behavior: An Introduction to Theory and Research.* Reading, Mass.: Addison-Wesley.

Garlington, W.
1977 Drinking on television: A preliminary study with emphasis on method. *Journal of Studies on Alcohol* 38:2199-2205.

Gerbner, G., Gross, L., Morgan, M., and Signorielli, N.
1981 Special report: Health and medicine on television. *The New England Journal of Medicine* 305(15):901-904.

Gerbner, G., Morgan, M., and Signorielli, N.
1982 Programming health portrayals: What viewers see, say and do. Pp. 291-307 in D. Pearl, L. Bouthilet, and J. Lazar, eds., *Television and Social Behavior: Ten Years of Scientific Progress and Implications for the Eighties*. Vol. II. Rockville, Md.: National Institute of Mental Health.

Gerstein, D.
1981 Alcohol use and consequences. Pp. 182-224 in M.H. Moore and D. Gerstein, eds., *Alcohol and Public Policy: Beyond the Shadow of Prohibition*. Washington, D.C.: National Academy Press.

Goldsen, R.
1980 The great American consciousness machine: Engineering the thought-environment. *Journal of Social Reconstruction* 1(2):87-102.

Gordon, N.P., and McAlister, A.L.
1982 Adolescent drinking: Issues and research. In T. Coates et al., eds., *Promoting Adolescent Health*. New York: Academic Press.

Governor's Task Force on Drunken Drivers
1982 Driving While Impaired: An Executive Response. North Carolina Department of Crime Control and Public Safety, Raleigh.

Green, L.W., Kreuter, M.S., Deeds, S.G., and Partridge, K.B.
1980 *Health Education Planning: A Diagnostic Approach*. Palo Alto, Calif.: Mayfield Publishing.

Greenberg, B.
1981 Television: Health issues on commerical television series. In M. Trudeau and M. Angle, eds., *Health Promotion and the Mass Media*. Washington, D.C.: National Academy Press.

Greenberg, B., Fernandez-Collado, C., Graef, D., Dorzenny F., and Atkin, C.
1979 *Trends in Use of Alcohol and Other Substances on Television*. East Lansing, Mich.: Department of Communication, Michigan State University.

Gusfield, J.
1976 The prevention of drinking problems. In J. Filstead, J. Rossi, and M. Keller, eds.,

Alcohol and Alcohol Problems: New Thinking and New Directions. Cambridge, Mass.: Ballinger.

Hamburg, B., and Pierce, C.
1982 Introductory comments. Pp. 288-290 in D. Pearl, L. Bouthilet, and J. Lazar, eds., *Television and Social Behavior: Ten Years of Scientific Progress and Implications for the Eighties.* Vol. II. Rockville, Md.: National Institute of Mental Health.

Harris, J.E.
1980 Taxing tar and nicotine. *American Economic Review* 70:300-311.
1982 Increasing the federal excise tax on cigarettes. *Journal of Health Economics* 1:117-120.

Jacobson, M., Hacker, G., and Atkins, R.
1983 *The Booze Merchants.* Washington, D.C.: Center for Science in the Public Interest.

Johnson, J.A., and Okanen, E.H.
1977 Estimates of demand for alcoholic beverages in Canada from pooled time series and cross sections. *Review of Economic and Statistics* 59(1):113-118.

Katzper, M., Ryback, R., and Hartzman, M.
1978 Alcohol beverage advertisement and consumption. *Journal of Drug Issues* 8:339-353.

Kelly, N.B.
1978 Health education through entertainment: A multimedia campaign. *Journal of the American College Health Association* 26:248-252.

Kraft, D.P.
In A comprehensive prevention program for college students. In P.M. Miller and
press T.D. Nirenberg, eds., *Prevention of Alcohol Abuse: Current Issues and Future Directions.* New York: Plenum.

Lelbach, K.
1974 Organic pathology related to volume and pattern of alcohol use. In R.J. Gibbons et al., eds., *Research Advances in Alcohol and Drug Problems.* Vol. 1. New York: Plenum.

Lewit, E., and Coate, D.
1982 The potential for using excise taxes to reduce smoking. *Journal of Health Economics* 1:121-146.

Lewit, E., Coate, D., and Grossman, M.
1981 The effects of government regulation on teenage smoking. *Journal of Law and Economics* 24:545-569.

Liquor Handbook
1981 New York: Gavin-Jobson Associates.

McAlister, A.L., and Edwards, M.
1983 General Coping Skills to Promote Adolescent Health and Development. Unpublished report prepared for the W.T. Grant Foundation, New York.

McAlister, A.L., Perry, C., Killen, J., Slinkard, L., and Maccoby, N.
1980 Pilot study of smoking, alcohol and drug abuse prevention. *American Journal of Public Health* 70:719-721.

McKinlay, J.
1979 A case for refocusing upstream: The political economy of illness. In E. Jaco, ed., *Patients, Physicians and Illness.* New York: The Free Press.

Medicine in the Public Interest
1979   *The Effect of Alcohol Beverage Control Laws.* Washington, D.C.: Medicine in the Public Interest.

Mello, N.K.
1972   Behavioral studies of alcoholism. In B. Kissin and K. Begleiter, eds., *The Biology of Alcoholism.* Vol. 2. New York: Plenum.

Milavsky, J., Kessler, R., Stipp, H., and Reubens, W.
1982   Television and aggression: Results of a panel study. Pp. 138-157 in D. Pearl, L. Bouthilet, and J. Lazar, eds., *Television and Social Behavior: Ten Years of Scientific Progress and Implications for the Eighties.* Vol. II. Rockville, Md.: National Institute of Mental Health.

Milio, N.
1976   A framework for prevention: Changing health-damaging to health-generating life patterns. *American Journal of Public Health* 66(5):435-439.

Monday Morning Report
1981   How much . . . *Monday Morning Report* August 31.

Moore, M.H., and Gerstein, D.R., eds.
1981   *Alcohol and Public Policy: Beyond the Shadow of Prohibition.* Panel on Alternative Policies Affecting the Prevention of Alcohol Abuse and Alcoholism. Washington, D.C.: National Academy Press.

Mosher, J.
1979   Dram shop liability and the prevention of alcohol-related programs. *Journal of Studies on Alcohol* 9:773-798.
1982   Dram shop liability and drunk driving: Toward an integrated approach to prevention. *Abstracts and Reviews in Alcohol & Driving* 3:3-6.
1983a   Alcoholic beverages as tax deductible business expenses: An issue of public health policy and prevention strategy. *Journal of Health Policy, Politics and Law* 7:855-888.
1983b   Server intervention: A new approach for preventing drinking-driving. *Accident Analysis and Prevention* 15(6):483-498.

Mosher, J., and Wallack, L.
1979a   *The DUI Project: Description of an Experimental Program to Address Drunk Driving Problems Conducted by the California Department of Alcoholic Beverage Control.* Sacramento, Calif.: California Department of Alcoholic Beverage Control.
1979b   Proposed reforms in the regulation of alcoholic beverage advertising. *Contemporary Drug Problems* 8:87-106.
1981   Government regulation of alcohol advertising: Protecting industry profits versus promoting the public health. *Journal of Public Health Policy* 2(4):333-353.

Nathan, P., and Lisman, S.
1976   Behavioral and motivational patterns of chronic alcoholics. In R. Tarter and A.A. Sugerman, eds., *Alcoholism: Interdisciplinary Approaches to an Enduring Problem.* Reading, Mass.: Addison-Wesley.

Neubauer, D., and Pratt, R.
1981   The second public health revolution: A critical appraisal. *Journal of Health Politics, Policy and Law* 6:205-288.

Ornstein, I., and Hanssens, D.M.
1981   Alcohol Control Laws, Consumer Welfare, and the Demand for Distilled Spirits

and Beer. Working Paper Series #102. Graduate School of Management, University of California, Los Angeles.

Peters, J.
1982 Bartending Is More Than Mixing Drinks. Unpublished manuscript. P.O. Box 165, Amherst, Mass.

Pittman, D., and Lambert, M.
1978 *Alcohol, Alcoholism and Advertising.* St. Louis, Mo.: Social Science Institute, Washington University.

Powell, W.J., Jr., and Klatskin, G.
1968 Duration of survival in patients with Laennec's cirrhosis. *American Journal of Medicine* 44:406-420.

Pratt, L.
1976 *Family Structure and Effective Health Behavior: The Energized Family.* Boston: Houghton Mifflin.

Ratcliffe, J., and Wallack, L.
1983 Primary Prevention in Public Health. Unpublished paper, School of Public Health, University of California, Berkeley.

Reed, D.
1981 Reducing the costs of drinking and driving. Pp. 336-387 in M. Moore and D. Gerstein, eds., *Alcohol and Public Policy: Beyond the Shadow of Prohibition.* Washington, D.C.: National Academy Press.

Rosenbluth, J., Nathan, P., and Lawson, D.
1978 Environmental influences on drinking by college students in a college pub: Behavioral observation in the natural environment. *Addictive Behaviors* 3:117-121.

Rubinstein, E.
1978 Television and the young viewer. *American Scientist* 66:685-693.

Ryan, B.E., and Segars, L.B.
1983 *First Conviction Program Population Description.* San Diego, Calif.: County of San Diego.

Schaefer, J.
1981 Bar Environments and Heavy Drinking. Talk presented at the Environmental Research Design Association annual meeting, Ames, Iowa.
1982 Supply Side Prevention. Unpublished manuscript, Alcohol and Other Drug Abuse Programming, St. Paul, Minn.

Schifrin, L.G.
1983 Societal costs of alcohol abuse in the United States: An updating. In M. Grant, M. Plant, and A. Williams, eds., *Economics and Alcohol.* New York: Gardner Press.

Schmidt, W.
1977 The epidemiology of cirrhosis of the liver: A statistical analysis of mortality with special reference to Canada. In M.M. Fisher and J.G. Rankin, eds., *Alcohol and the Liver.* New York: Plenum.

Seeley, J.R.
1960 Death by liver cirrhosis and the price of beverage alcohol. *Canadian Medical Association Journal* 83:1361-1366.

Sherif, M., and Sherif, C.W.
1974 *Reference Groups: Exploration Into Conformity and Deviation of Adolescents.* New York: Harper and Row.

Shold, R., and Morgan, R.
1982 Bartender alcohol awareness program. *Abstracts and Reviews in Alcohol and Driving* 3:15-19.

Signorielli, N., Gross, L., and Morgan, M.
1982 Violence in television programs: Ten years later. Pp. 158-174 in D. Pearl, L. Bouthilet, and J. Lazar, eds., *Television and Social Behavior: Ten Years of Scientific Progress and Implications for the Eighties*. Vol. II. Rockville, Md.: National Institute of Mental Health.

Skog, O.J.
1979 Drinking Behavior in Small Groups: The Relationship Between Group Size and Consumption Level. Paper presented at the workshop on Conceptual and Methodological Aspects of Drinking Contexts, Washington, D.C. Mimeograph 26, National Institute for Alcohol Research, Oslo.

Stepnick, L.
1983 Dram Shop Legislation in North Carolina: What It Should Look Like, How It Should Work. Unpublished manuscript, Department of Economics, Duke University.

Strickland, D.E.
1982a Alcohol advertising: Content and controversy. *Journal of Advertising* 1:223-236.
1982b Alcohol advertising: Orientations and influence. *Journal of Advertising* 1:307-319.

Strickland, D.E., Finn, T.A., and Lambert, M.D.
1982 A content analysis of beverage alcohol advertising: Magazine advertising. *Journal of Studies on Alcohol* 43(7):655-682.

Swedish Council for Information on Alcohol and Other Drugs
1982 *Alcohol Policy in Sweden—A Survey by the Swedish Council for Information on Alcohol and Other Drugs*. Stockholm: Swedish Council for Information on Alcohol and Other Drugs.

U.S. Senate
1976 *Media Images of Alcohol: The Effects of Advertising and Other Media on Alcohol Abuse, 1976*. Subcommittee on Alcoholism and Narcotics, Committee on Labor and Public Welfare. Available from the Superintendent of Documents, U.S. Government Printing Office, Washington, D.C.

Wagenaar, A.
1982 Aggregate beer and wine consumption: Effect of changes in the minimum legal drinking age and a mandatory beverage container deposit law in Michigan. *Journal of Studies on Alcohol* 43:469-488.

Wallack, L.
1981 Mass media campaigns: The odds against finding behavior change. *Health Education Quarterly* 8(3):209-260.
1982 An Application of the Systems Approach to the Prevention of Alcohol-Related Problems: A Case Study of a Mass Media Campaign. Unpublished dissertation, School of Public Health, University of California, Berkeley.
In   Public health and the prevention of alcohol problems. In H. Holder and J. Hallan,
press eds., *Control Issues in Alcohol Abuse*. Columbia: University of South Carolina Press.

Waring, M., and Spier, I.
1982 Bartenders: An untapped resource for the prevention of alcohol abuse? *International Journal of Addictions* 17:859-868.

White House Conference on Families
1980   Listening to America's Families: Action for the 80s. Report to the President,
       Congress and Families of the Nation, October.

Wine Marketing Handbook
1981   New York: Gavin-Jobson Associates.

Winick, C., and Winick, P.
1976   Drug education and the content of mass media dealing with "dangerous drugs"
       and alcohol. Pp. 15-38 in R. Ostman, ed., *Communication Research and Drug
       Education*. Beverly Hills, Calif.: Sage Publications.

Wittman, F.
1980   *Tale of Two Cities: Policies and Practices in the Local Control of Alcohol Avail-
       ability*. Berkeley, Calif.: Alcohol Research Group.
1982   *Community Perspectives on the Prevention of Alcohol Problems*. Berkeley, Calif.:
       Prevention Research Group, Medical Research Institute of San Francisco.

Wolfe, A.
1974   1973 U.S. national roadside breathtaking survey. *Hit Lab Reports* 4(11). Ann
       Arbor, Mich.: Highway Safety Research Institute, University of Michigan.

Worden, M.
1979   Popular and unpopular prevention. *Journal of Drug Abuse* Summer:425-433.

World Almanac & Book of Facts, 1982
1981   New York: Newspaper Enterprise Association, Inc.

Wynne, J.D.
1982a *Analysis of Inebriate Reception Center Utilization*. San Diego, Calif.: County of
       San Diego.
1982b *Public Inebriety in San Diego*. San Diego, Calif.: County of San Diego.

Yoder, R.
1975   Prearrest behavior of persons convicted of driving while intoxicated. *Journal of
       Studies on Alcohol* 36:1573-1577.

Participants

CONFERENCE ON ALCOHOL AND
PUBLIC POLICY
May 20-21, 1983

GAIL BURTON ALLEN, Department of Psychiatry, St. Luke's-
Roosevelt Hospital Center, New York
CATHERINE ANDERSON, National Program Underwriting,
Metropolitan Pittsburgh Public Broadcasting, Inc.
DAN E. BEAUCHAMP, School of Public Health, University of North
Carolina
MARILYN BEGGS, Vice President, Region V, National Parent-Teacher
Association, Lincoln, Nebraska
BEVERLY BLAKEY, Commission on Behavioral and Social Sciences
and Education, National Research Council
SHEILA BLUME, National Council on Alcoholism, New York
BERNELL N. BOSWELL, School on Alcohol and Other Drug
Dependencies, University of Utah
SISTER MADELEINE BOYD, SND, Shalom Inc., Philadelphia
EDWARD BRECHER, West Cornwall, Connecticut
PETER BROCK, Johnson Institute, Minneapolis
WILLIAM BUTYNSKI, National Association of State Alcohol and Drug
Abuse Directors, Washington, D.C.
THEA CHALOW, WGBH-TV Public Broadcasting, Boston
STANLEY COHEN, Washington Bureau, *Advertising Age*
PHILIP COOK, Institute of Policy Sciences and Public Affairs, Duke
University
CHARLES CRAWFORD, Ernest and Julio Gallo Winery, Modesto,
California

171

JOHN DOYLE, National Council on Alcoholism, New York

RIPLEY FORBES, Subcommittee on Health and the Environment, Committee on Energy and Commerce, U.S. House of Representatives

BARBARA FORDE, Research Department, National School Boards Association, Washington, D.C.

MICHAEL FOX, Ohio General Assembly, Columbus

PAUL GAVAGHAN, Distilled Spirits Council of the United States, Inc., Washington, D.C.

MINDY GAYNES, National Conference of State Legislatures, Denver

DEAN GERSTEIN, Commission on Behavioral and Social Sciences and Education, National Research Council

STEPHEN GODWIN, Transportation Research Board, National Research Council

MARILYN GOLDWATER, Maryland House of Delegates, Annapolis

MICHAEL GOODSTADT, Alcoholism and Drug Addiction Research Foundation, Toronto

GEORGE HACKER, Center for Science in the Public Interest, Washington, D.C.

CLAY HALL, Office of Alcohol Countermeasures, National Highway Traffic Safety Administration

JEFFREY E. HARRIS, Department of Economics, Massachusetts Institute of Technology, and Massachusetts General Hospital

MARGARET HASTINGS, Illinois Commission on Mental Health and Developmental Disabilities, Chicago

GAIL HEALY, White House Office of Drug Policy

MARY HEVENER, Tax Policy Office, U.S. Department of the Treasury

ALAN KAPLAN, Washington, D.C.

MARK KELLER, The Center of Alcohol Studies, Rutgers University

FRANK KENEL, Office of Traffic Safety, American Automobile Association, Falls Church, Virginia

JOHN KENNY, New York City Police Department

HENRY KING, United States Brewers Association, Washington, D.C.

DAVID P. KRAFT, University Health Services, University of Massachusetts, Amherst

EDWARD J. KUNEC, Mothers Against Drunk Drivers, Northern Virginia

MILDRED LEHMAN, Alcohol, Drug Abuse, and Mental Health Administration, U.S. Department of Health and Human Services

JAY LEWIS, Public Policy Office, National Council on Alcoholism, Washington, D.C.

CHRIS LUBINSKI, Subcommittee on Alcoholism and Drug Abuse, Committee on Labor and Human Resources, U.S. Senate

KLAUS MÄKELÄ, Social Research Institute of Alcohol Studies, The State Alcohol Monopoly, Helsinki

BEN MASON, Adolph Coors Company, Golden, Colorado

WILLIAM MAYER, Alcohol, Drug Abuse, and Mental Health Administration, U.S. Department of Health and Human Services

ALFRED MCALISTER, Center for Health Promotion, University of Texas Health Sciences Center, Houston

DONALD MCCONNELL, Commission on Alcohol and Drug Abuse, State of Connecticut

MICHAEL MCGINNIS, Health Promotion and Disease Prevention, U.S. Department of Health and Human Services

ROBERT MCKEAGNEY, Department of Human Services, State of Maine

MARK H. MOORE, John F. Kennedy School of Government, Harvard University

JAMES F. MOSHER, Prevention Research Group, Medical Research Institute of San Francisco

WALTER MURPHY, National Council on Alcoholism, New York

FRANK PADAVAN, New York State Senate

JANE SMITH PATTERSON, Department of Administration, State of North Carolina

LORNE PHILLIPS, Alcohol and Drug Abuse Services, State Department of Social and Rehabilitation Services, Topeka

FRANK RAFLO, Board of Supervisors, County of Loudoun, Virginia

ROBERT REYNOLDS, Department of Health Services-Alcohol Program, County of San Diego

ROBERT A. ROSS, Division of Alcoholism and Alcohol Abuse, State of New York

PATRICIA SCHNEIDER, Wine Institute, San Francisco

KEITH SCHUCHARD, Parental Resource Institute for Drug Education, Atlanta

SHARMAN STEVENS, Office of the Assistant Secretary for Planning and Evaluation, U.S. Department of Health and Human Services

LARRY STEWART, Laurland Productions and Caucus of Producers, Writers, and Directors, Los Angeles

ROBERT STRAUS, Department of Behavioral Sciences, College of Medicine, University of Kentucky

BARRY SWEEDLER, Bureau of Safety Programs, National Transportation Safety Board

DIANA TABLER, Office of the Administrator, Alcohol, Drug Abuse, and Mental Health Administration

RICK THEIS, Office of Public Affairs, Wine Spectrum, Atlanta

ROGER THOMSON, S & A Restaurant Corporation, Dallas

THOMAS TURNER, Johns Hopkins Alcohol Research Center, Baltimore
JOHN F. VASSALLO, JR., Division of Alcoholic Beverage Control, State of New Jersey, Trenton
LAWRENCE WALLACK, School of Public Health, University of California, Berkeley
FRIEDNER WITTMAN, Prevention Research Group, Medical Research Institute of San Francisco
NANCY WOLICKI, Subcommittee on Alcoholism and Drug Abuse, Committee on Labor and Human Resources, U.S. Senate
JEFFREY WYNNE, Department of Health Services-Alcohol Program, County of San Diego

NATIONAL INSTITUTE ON ALCOHOL ABUSE AND ALCOHOLISM

LORAN ARCHER, Deputy Director
FRAN COTTER, Office of Policy Analysis
SUSAN FARRELL, Office of Policy Analysis
JUDI FUNKHOUSER, Prevention Branch
BRENDA HEWITT, Special Assistant to the Director
STEVEN LONG, Financial Management and Budget Office
BARBARA LUBRAN, Planning Branch
JOHN NOBLE, Division of Biometry and Epidemiology
ALBERT PAWLOWSKI, National Centers Branch
GIAN C. SALMOIRAGHI, Office of Scientific Affairs
LEE TOWLE, International and Intergovernmental Affairs
JEANNE TRUMBLE, The Secretary's Initiative on Teenage Alcohol Abuse
JOAN WHITE, Office of Policy Analysis